BAKE &
decorate

FIONA CAIRNS

cover and interior photographs by Laura Hynd

RODALE®

For Kishore, Hari and Tara, with my love.
Thanks for giving me your summer.

CONTENTS

bake

decorate

Baking and eating cakes and cookies is all about home, comfort, pleasure and luxury. Admittedly, they are not an essential part of our daily diet or sustenance, but they are vital to our souls. Cakes are a treat. They can be a gift, an occasion in their own right to be shared while relaxing around a kitchen table, eaten indulgently solo, or given as a centerpiece at a lavish celebration with loved ones. For me, they are also about the unmistakeable sweet aroma of the oven, the light texture of a cake crumb or the tantalizing fragrance of citrus and rose water in a syrup.

Cakes create memories. I'd like our children to have those memories, too. For many of us, baking was our first introduction to the kitchen and I remember fighting over scraping down and licking the mixing bowl with my brother. Even now, I have been known to sneak the last drop of some silky, melted, still-warm chocolate. Sadly, in our increasingly busy lives, many of us these days lack the time and knowledge to bake. I want to change that. I hope to show in this book that the process of baking and decorating is just as enjoyable as the eating; it might surprise you. Everyone makes mistakes, even the professionals, so a lack of confidence is no reason not to give it a try. Once, when making Christmas cakes, I lost an earring in the batter. I only found it with the help of a metal detector!

You will find some very simple recipes in this book clearly explained, which you can decorate or not, depending on your mood and the occasion. If this is all new to you, try something easy at first – maybe a Victoria Sponge Cake, or one of my recipes that require no cooking, such as sumptuous Gilded Chocolate Tiffin – and progress from there.

Baking differs from other types of cookery because it really is all about exact measurements, basic rules and oven temperatures. This means you do need to follow the recipes in the Bake chapter closely. All of them will stand you in excellent stead for the rest of your baking life ahead. You may find new, sophisticated favorites, such as my exotic, headily scented Star Anise, Almond and Clementine Cake, or turn to the warmth of classics such as an impeccable carrot cake. All the recipes work perfectly; once you have followed the instructions, you will always have a successful and delicious cake that tastes wonderful. Don't worry; the bossy part is over now!

The creations in the Decorate chapter – all made from my Bake recipes – are there to spark your own imagination. They are intended as a starting point. If I have inspired you to try some of the ideas or, even better, to find new ways to express your own creativity, and you find yourself wondering what to try next, then I have succeeded. Do also have a look at my 25 Easy Cheats, which will help you to conjure up a fabulous cake with a minimum of fuss, cost or effort.

Cake decorating can seem daunting, but this book is certainly not. Few of the decorated cakes require special equipment, previous knowledge, or masses of time. Some use the everyday objects we are surrounded with, such as candies, ribbons or fresh flowers, in imaginative ways. They will let you rediscover the ancient pleasures to be had from crafting something beautiful with your hands.

As you improve in confidence and skill, your reputation will grow. You'll become known as the best baker in town for glamorous desserts and trusted to make a stunning cake with elegance and charm.

Parents will find new ways to lift a child's birthday party into a wild success; try making quirky Flying Insect cupcakes or even baking delightful Ice-cream Cones, cakes that won't melt in the sun.

If parties are more your thing, hold a spring celebration with a White Chocolate and Cardamom Rose Water Cake that will have guests clamoring for the recipe, or produce a table laden with Doily Cookies, Sticky Ginger Cake and Chile Chocolate Cupcakes to bring comfort to a winter afternoon. You could even offer something a little stronger alongside the pots of tea and coffee!

Whatever your style, my book will help you create the perfect, most delicious occasion for your friends and family, where the cake is the star and the baker glows in its reflected warmth. Happy baking!

ingredients guide

As in all cooking, the better the ingredients, the more delicious the results, so do not stint. Buy the best you can afford.

butter
I use unsalted butter and so do these recipes. The exception is where I specify salted butter, such as for my Classic Shortbread (page 74). I never use margarine. Margarine gives a light cake, as it has already been whipped, but if you follow my instructions for creaming butter you will have a feather-light cake with a far superior flavor.

chocolate
This subject is a minefield. These days we're faced with an array of high-quality chocolates with varying percentages and it can be daunting. The percentage indicates the amount of cacao solids in the chocolate. In these recipes I indicate the best type to use. Where I specify milk chocolate, use a bar with at least 30% cacao solids. With white chocolate, buy a brand that uses cocoa butter and not other tropical fats.

citrus
Use unwaxed, organic citrus whenever possible, especially if you are using the zest.

dulche de leche
A delicious caramel sauce from Argentina, found in jars in most supermarkets.

eggs
Do use organic or free-range eggs. I use large, and all the recipes in this book assume you do, too.

flour
I use unbleached flour as I find it has more flavor; it is purer and free from chemicals. Organic flour has a fuller flavor.

fondant
This makes covering and decorating cakes so easy. It is widely available, and I don't think it's worth making yourself. Once kneaded, fondant becomes pliable and gives cakes a lovely smooth finish. It is great for forming shapes, too; a bit like children's modeling clay. It comes in a range of colors, but I prefer to mix my own more interesting shades.

molasses and golden syrup
Far easier to measure if you first oil the measuring spoon, or dip it into boiling water.

nuts
Buy little and often, as they turn rancid very quickly. Please make a point of roasting them, as I suggest in the recipes; it makes a huge difference as it releases their oils. Any leftover nuts freeze well.

rose water and orange flower water
Widely available from supermarkets, but try to buy from a Middle Eastern shop if you can, as the fragrance is more intense (so use a smaller amount).

spices
Buy small amounts and store them in a dark cupboard. Grate fresh nutmeg as needed; the flavor is incomparable to pre-ground.

sugar
Organic raw sugar has much more flavor; do try to use finely granulated organic raw sugar instead of white (except for snowy white meringues). Brown muscovado sugars are quite delicious; their taste and color come from the molasses clinging to the grains. Light muscovado has a butterscotch flavor and creams very well. Dark muscovado has a strong flavor that could overpower, but its deep taste is perfect in rich fruit cakes. If it hardens (it will if the packet is left open), empty it into an ovenproof dish, cover and warm at a very low oven temperature.

vanilla
Use only pure vanilla extract or vanilla beans. Always avoid anything labelled "vanilla flavor" as it is synthetic and doesn't taste at all like the real thing. A good habit to get into is to make vanilla sugar. Stick 3–4 vanilla beans into a jar of sugar and leave for a week or two. Add more as required. This is invaluable for baking or sprinkling on to shortbreads, cakes and fruits.

equipment guide

buttercream

1⅓ cups unsalted butter, softened
4 cups confectioners' sugar, sifted

In an electric mixer, beat the butter until really pale and fluffy. Add your flavor and the sugar and beat for at least 5 minutes, until light and creamy.

flavorings

vanilla 2 teaspoons vanilla extract or seeds of
    1 vanilla bean
chocolate 3½ ounces 70% cacao solids chocolate,
    melted and cooled, or 2 tablespoons cocoa
    powder, sifted
coffee 2 tablespoons strong-brewed black coffee
raspberry/blueberry/strawberry 4 tablespoons fresh
    fruit puree (not too wet)
lemon/orange/lime zest of 2 fruits, finely grated,
    and juice of 1, added slowly at the end
liqueur 1 tablespoon, added slowly at the end
nut 1 cup roasted nuts, ground and cooled

cupcake and mini muffin pans

There is an ever-increasing array on the market, and it is seriously confusing. The sizes and names vary and, therefore, will alter how many you can make in a batch and their cooking times. The instructions I have given worked for me and are approximate. As a general rule, the very small pans are called "mini muffin" pans. The next size up are called "muffin," then the very large "Texas" or "jumbo."

oven

Ovens vary enormously: no two are the same and you are very familiar with yours. It is very useful to have an oven thermometer, to check if yours is too cool or too hot. Always preheat the oven and have the racks at the correct heights. (Bake a cake in the center of a convection oven, or on the top shelf of a conventional oven.) This way, you won't have your cakes sitting around while you fiddle with the racks and lose valuable heat...sound familiar?

pans

There is a huge variety on the market; buy the best you can. Really good-quality pans will last many years, conduct heat well and won't warp. Nonstick, loose-bottomed or springform pans make baking so much easier. Try to use the size of pan specified. If you don't have the correct size, err on the side of a slightly larger pan (the cake will be shallower) and reduce the baking time by 5 to 10 minutes.

parchment paper

I use nonstick parchment paper for lining pans. It is essential for meringues; they stick to wax paper.

piping cones

Here is how to make a piping cone from parchment paper for royal icing. Remember you'll need to buy nylon, washable bags for piping buttercream and meringues.

Start with a 12" square of parchment paper. Fold in half to form a double-thickness triangle. Place it with the tip pointing away from you. The center of the long side nearest you will form the tip where the icing will come out (and where you put a nozzle). Twist the parchment around to form a cone, then secure with your thumb and forefinger. Adjust the layers until the cone has a sharp tip. (When using more than 2 ounces of icing, make a bigger cone.)

Fold all the overlapping papers inside the cone twice to secure. Cut 2 little snips ½" apart in the folds to hold the seam, then fold back this tab. Only ever half-fill a bag, and fold shut the open end. Snip off the tip with scissors to make the opening as large as you need.

royal icing

4 teaspoons dried egg whites
2⅔ cups confectioners' sugar, sifted

Using an electric mixer, beat the dried egg whites with ¼ cup water until foaming. Gradually beat in the sugar. Continue for 2 minutes. The consistency is key; it must hold its shape when piped. If needed, add more water to thin, or sugar to thicken.

scales and measurements

Baking is an exact science. Measure everything precisely. Use solid cups for dry ingredients and transparent cups for liquids.

baking tips

As I have said in the ingredients section (see page 8), once you have good-quality components, you're halfway there!

read the recipe
Always read right to the end and only then assemble all the ingredients and equipment you need. This makes life easier, less stressful, and more enjoyable.

temperature of mixing bowls and ingredients
A warm kitchen, equipment and ingredients make a great cake. So, when baking a cake, stand your mixing bowl and beater or whisk in a bowl of warm water, then dry thoroughly before you start. Conversely, cooler ingredients and temperatures result in perfect cookies. Hence, marble and cold hands are good for making them. Is this why Scottish shortbreads are so famous?

Try to think ahead and remove eggs and butter from the refrigerator an hour before. But, if the urge to bake suddenly strikes, stand the eggs in a bowl of warm water, and soften the butter in a microwave.

creaming butter and sugar
I have usually suggested 5 minutes to cream the butter and sugar - both for a cake and for buttercream - and, should you time yourself, you will see it is quite a while. The reason is that there is a very noticeable difference: the color changes and the mixture becomes aerated as it increases in volume, turning pale and fluffy. Keep scraping the sides of your bowl with a spatula during the process to make sure all ingredients are well blended in.

light as air
When sifting flour, lift the sieve up high; this allows air to coat the particles of flour as they float down.

lining pans
While the bottoms of cake pans are always lined with parchment paper, in many cases the sides only need to be buttered. The exception is if you're baking a cake that will be in the oven a long time (such as a fruit cake), when it will help protect the sides. If at all in doubt, line the sides with parchment, too.

don't hang around...
Once a cake's in the pan, bake it immediately as, when moistened, the leavenings start to work. (A dense fruit cake batter isn't so sensitive.)

...but be patient!
Don't be tempted to open the oven door to peep at your cake too often, and wait until the final 5 to 10 minutes. If you keep opening the door at the start, you will affect the rise and texture of the cake.

when is it ready?
Insert a wooden toothpick into the very center of your cake. If it emerges clean, the cake is cooked. Long-baked fruit cakes may need extra attention: cut a piece of foil to fit the surface. Pierce a hole in the center and open it up. This lets out steam while protecting the surface from drying out or scorching.

disaster management
—You only need to lose the bottom half of a sticky or fragile cake to a wire rack once; in future, you'll place a sheet of baking parchment on first.
—If your cake isn't cooked in the middle or has sunk, all is not lost. Dig out and discard the middle then fill the resulting hole with cream and berries.
—On New Year's Eve (after the shops closed) I made a very large chocolate cake for a party. I took it from the oven too soon; it was raw inside. So I cut out rounds (avoiding the center), decorated with gold leaf and arranged on a platter. No one knew.
—When adding eggs to creamed butter and sugar, do so very slowly, as the batter can otherwise curdle. If it does, just carry on. The cake may not rise as it should, but will taste delicious.
—If your cake is very dry, douse it with a dessert or fortified wine and use it as the base for a trifle.

a note on perfect cookies
When rolling out, cut the shapes as close together as possible so you are not re-rolling too often (or the dough will toughen). When ready, cookies will look darker but may seem underdone. They aren't. They will crisp up. Always space cookies out on the baking sheet at least ½" apart, as they spread.

decorating tips

sculpting and shaping
If cutting up a cake, a short spell (1 hour) in the refrigerator or freezer makes it easier to shape.

icing
be generous You'll always need more marzipan or fondant; start with the amounts specified.
cool it Always make sure the cake is absolutely cold, or it will be soggy and the icing will not stick.

get the foundations right
Turn the cake upside down so the base becomes a flat top. Cracks or blemishes can be filled in with buttercream, fondant, or marzipan.

fondant
Knead to make it pliable and, if it is too sticky, dust your hands and work surface with confectioners' sugar. If it dries, add a tiny amount of vegetable shortening. Use a food processor with a dough blade, to save your muscles. Store in a sealed plastic bag at room temperature (never the refrigerator).

When rolling it out, dust a work surface and rolling pin with confectioners' sugar and frequently run a metal spatula underneath. It's very frustrating if it sticks to the surface. Never store a fondant-covered cake or decorations in the refrigerator. When covering a cake, ensure your rolled-out fondant is slightly larger than the cake and sides, and wrap it loosely around the rolling pin before smoothing it on to the cake. If there are air bubbles, prick them with a pin and rub away the hole. Once a cake is covered, store in a cardboard box, not an airtight container as it will sweat. Avoid contact with water, which will mark it.

coloring fondant
Color the fondant the day before you need it, as it will be easier to roll and shape. Dip the end of a toothpick into food coloring paste and drag it across the fondant. Knead until it's an even color and you achieve the desired shade. If you need different tones, make the darker first then lighten with white fondant, or it's hard to get the same shade. With strong colors, wear gloves to protect your hands.

food coloring
Use food coloring paste, not liquid, where you can. In either case, food colors can be a little unsubtle, so mix them up for a more interesting palette. A pinprick of brown, even black, works wonders. They are intense, so you'll only need a very small amount.

adding ribbons
Secure ribbons with a dab of icing at the back, as it will dry to leave a mark which should be hidden.

hiding flaws
Many designs in this book are very forgiving. Any blemishes can be covered with a decoration.

transporting decorated cakes
Cakes are more robust than you may think and most transport easily. When taking a cake to a venue, err on the side of caution and take a repair kit - a bag of royal icing and a few spare decorations - in the rare event that something has fallen off or broken. It is really important that cakes are stored in dry conditions at room temperature.

cutting a fruit cake
There's an art to cutting fruit cake, as it can crumble. Use a very sharp or serrated knife. Place the blade right across the cake and, with a gentle sawing action, cut into slices. Wipe the knife between each cut with paper towels. The knife won't become sticky and the icing will remain clean.

a note on freezing
As a rule, a cake is at its best freshly baked, although many will keep well for a few days and fruit cakes need time to mature.

After one of the shoots for this book, I took the Rose Garden Cake (page 109) to my neighbor, in its full finery, adorned with crystallized roses. She told me later that she had frozen the whole cake (roses and all) for the weekend. I must have sounded sceptical, as she brought the remains for me to see; she and her family found the cake delicious and the roses were intact. I write this because, although I am not keen on freezing cakes, it seems it can work!

bake

chocolate celebration cake

This is a really dark chocolate cake, perfect for a big occasion. It's also moist enough to serve as a dessert with crème fraiche and berries. This is a large amount of cake but, for a smaller party, use exactly half the recipe to fill a 9" round springform pan and bake for just 25–35 minutes.

Lightly butter a 12" springform pan and line the bottom with parchment paper. Preheat the oven to 350°F.

Set a large heatproof bowl over a saucepan of very gently simmering water, making sure the bottom of the bowl does not touch the water. Dissolve the coffee in 1/4 cup boiling water. Add the coffee, chocolate, sugar, and butter to the bowl and melt together. Cool a little, then add the flour and mix well until smooth. Add the egg yolks, one at a time, mixing between each addition.

Whisk the egg whites with the salt to stiff peaks. Using a large spoon or spatula, fold a big spoonful of egg whites into the chocolate mixture. Once combined, fold in the rest. Pour into the pan, smooth the top and bake for 40–45 minutes, or until firm to the touch and a wooden toothpick inserted into the center comes out clean. The sides will just be beginning to shrink from the pan.

Remove from the oven, leave in the pan for about 5 minutes. Turn out on to a wire rack, remove the paper, and cool completely.

For the ganache, melt the chocolate, cream and butter in a heatproof bowl set over simmering water, again ensuring the bottom of the bowl does not touch the water. Stir until smooth, then cool a little to thicken before pouring over the cake. Let set for at least 2 hours.

SERVES 16–20

FOR THE CAKE
4 teaspoons instant coffee
14 ounces bittersweet chocolate (70% cacao), chopped
1 1/3 cups organic sugar
11 tablespoons unsalted butter, cubed, plus more for the pan
3/4 cup plus 1 tablespoon self-rising flour, sifted
10 large eggs, separated
1/2 teaspoon salt

FOR THE GANACHE
7 ounces bittersweet chocolate (70% cacao), chopped
1/3 cup heavy cream
4 tablespoons unsalted butter

TO DECORATE see: 23-carat Gold Cake, page 82; Bollywood Extravaganza, page 126; Chile Chocolate Cupcakes, page 167

family chocolate cake

Buttermilk helps to lighten the texture and adds flavor.

Preheat the oven to 350°F. Butter two 8" round cake pans, and line the bottoms with parchment paper.

Place the chocolate in a bowl and pour in 6 tablespoons boiling water. Stir until melted, then set aside to cool.

In a bowl, sift together the flour, baking powder, and baking soda, then stir in the ground almonds. In the bowl of an electric mixer (or in a bowl with a electric hand mixer), cream together the butter and sugar until very light and fluffy (this will take a good 5 minutes). Add the vanilla extract to the eggs. With the whisk running, very slowly add the egg mixture to the butter and sugar, adding 1 tablespoon of the flour during the process to prevent curdling, then add the melted chocolate and the buttermilk.

Fold in the remaining flour very gently. Divide the mixture between the pans. Bake for 30–35 minutes, or until firm to the touch. Leave for a minute or 2 in the pans before turning out on to a wire rack. Remove the papers and leave until absolutely cold.

To make the icing, melt the chocolate and butter in a heatproof bowl over gently simmering water. Make sure the bottom of the bowl does not touch the water. Remove the bowl from the heat, then stir in the syrup and sugar. Gradually pour in the cream until all is well blended and smooth. Let cool completely, then whisk until it thickens. Spread half on the base of 1 cake. Sandwich the 2 cakes, bases together, then spread the remaining icing on top.

SERVES 8

FOR THE CAKE
3½ ounces semisweet chocolate (50–60% cacao), finely chopped
1⅓ cups all-purpose flour
1 teaspoon baking powder
1 teaspoon baking soda
1 cup almond flour
¾ cup unsalted butter, softened, plus more for the pan
1⅓ cups packed brown sugar
1 teaspoon vanilla extract
3 large eggs, lightly beaten
½ cup buttermilk

FOR THE FUDGE ICING
3 ounces semisweet chocolate (50–60% cacao), chopped
3 tablespoons unsalted butter, softened and diced
1 tablespoon golden syrup
2 tablespoons packed brown sugar
½ cup heavy cream

TO DECORATE see: Sweet Shop, page 96; Party Cake with Streamers, page 119; Chocolate Spiral, page 144; Mint Cupcakes, page 164; Parcels, page 170

white chocolate and cardamom rose water cake

This is very delicately flavored and the tastes of white chocolate, cardamom, and rose water marry beautifully. White chocolate ganache, which forms the filling, can be tricky. I've had my best success using Swiss white chocolate.

Preheat the oven to 350°F. I make this cake in a heart-shaped pan measuring 9¹/₂" at its widest point and 2¹/₂" deep, but otherwise use an 8" springform pan. Butter the pan very well, then line the bottom with parchment paper.

Grind the cardamom pods: split them with the point of a knife, empty out the little seeds and grind them to a powder in a mortar and pestle. There may be a few pieces of husk mixed in, so sift the cardamom powder together with the flour to remove them.

Place the chocolate in a food processor with half the sugar. Process until as fine as possible. Take 2 tablespoons hot tap water and let cool until you can just dip in your finger. Dribble it into the chocolate, processing until most has melted. Add the remaining sugar and the butter, cut into tablespoons, and process well. Add the eggs, flour, and vanilla and mix again. Don't worry if there are tiny pieces of chocolate left in the batter.

Pour into the pan and bake for 25–30 minutes or until a wooden toothpick comes out clean. Cool in the pan for a few minutes, then turn out on to a wire rack, removing the papers. Let cool completely.

Meanwhile, make the ganache. Place the chocolate in a bowl. In a saucepan, bring the cream and rose water to the boil. Pour the cream over the chocolate, let stand for a few seconds, then gently stir until smooth. Let cool. Chill slightly, then whisk until it thickens.

Split the cake in half and invert so the flat base forms the top. Fill with the ganache and top with the second layer of cake. Place the confectioners' sugar in a small bowl and stir in 1¹/₂–2 tablespoons water until thick enough to coat the back of a spoon. Pour it over the cake, allowing it to drizzle down the sides.

TO DECORATE see: A Summer Garden, page 99; Rose Petal Heart, page 102

SERVES 8

FOR THE CAKE
20 green cardamom pods
3¹/₂ ounces white chocolate, chopped
²/₃ cup superfine sugar
9 tablespoons unsalted butter, softened, plus more for the pan
1 cup plus 3 tablespoons self-rising flour
2 large eggs, beaten
1 teaspoon vanilla extract

FOR THE GANACHE
3¹/₂ ounces white chocolate, finely chopped
¹/₃ cup heavy cream
2 teaspoons rose water

FOR THE ICING
¹/₃ cup confectioners' sugar, sifted

chocolate and beet cake

Beet juice is a natural dye that gives an amazing pink, and we use it a lot in the bakery. Here it stains the icing instead of the usual synthetic food coloring. But, if you want an even brighter pink, cheat and add a little food coloring, too. And please, whatever you do, don't use canned beets! To cook the beets, wrap each in aluminum foil and place on a baking sheet. Bake at 400°F until tender, about 1 hour. Cool and peel before using.

Preheat the oven to 350°F. Lightly oil a 9" springform pan, using a piece of paper towel, then line the bottom with parchment paper.

In a large bowl, sift together the flour, cocoa and baking soda, then stir in the sugar. In a food processor, purée the beets, then scrape into a sieve set over a bowl and push out the juices with the back of a spoon. Set the juice aside for the icing. Return the beet pulp to the food processor, then, with the motor running, add the eggs and vanilla, then slowly pour in the oil. Mix until blended.

Make a well in the center of the dry ingredients, pour in the beet mixture and, with a large spoon, gently fold together. Pour into the pan. Bake for 45–50 minutes or until a wooden toothpick inserted into the center comes out clean. If it starts to brown too much, cut a round piece of aluminum foil to fit the top, make a large hole in the center and open it up. Place it over the cake to let out steam and protect the edges of the top surface.

Remove the cake from the oven and let cool for 5–10 minutes in the pan, then turn it out on to a wire rack, remove the paper and cool completely.

Sift the confectioners' sugar into a bowl. Stir in a few tablespoons of the reserved beet juice and, depending on how bright you want the color, a little pink food coloring (if you like). The icing should be thick enough to coat the back of a spoon. If not, add water, 1/2 teaspoon at a time, until you achieve the correct consistency.

Turn the cake over, so the bottom becomes a flat top. Spread the icing evenly over, letting it drizzle down the sides.

TO DECORATE see: Abstract Expressionist, page 84

SERVES 10

FOR THE CAKE
1⅓ cups self-rising flour
⅔ cup natural cocoa powder
1 teaspoon baking soda
1¼ cups organic sugar
9 ounces beets, cooked
3 large eggs
1 teaspoons vanilla extract
⅔ cup sunflower oil, plus more for the pan

FOR THE ICING
1¾ cups confectioners' sugar
pink food coloring (optional)

flourless chocolate
hazelnut cake

This is the perfect cake for those on a gluten-free diet. Feel free to experiment with other nuts, as both almonds or pecans would be as good as hazelnuts. For a more festive presentation, serve with raspberry sauce. You can leave out the ganache if you prefer, and simply decorate the top with the raspberries dusted with confectioners' sugar.

Preheat the oven to 350°F. Butter an 8 x 1½" round cake pan, and line the bottom with parchment paper.

Roast the hazelnuts in the oven for 5–10 minutes, watching carefully so they don't burn. Let cool. Grind finely in a food processor. Place the chocolate, ⅓ cup of the sugar and the butter in a heatproof bowl set over very gently simmering water (ensure the bottom of the bowl does not touch the water) and melt together gently. Remove from the heat and stir in the hazelnuts. Beat the egg yolks until they thicken and turn pale yellow, then fold them into the cooled chocolate mixture.

In another, very clean bowl, whisk the egg whites until foamy, then slowly beat in the remaining sugar until soft peaks form. Take a large spoonful and fold it into the chocolate to lighten it. Then fold in the remaining egg whites, as gently and lightly as you can, using a large spatula. Transfer the batter to the pan. Bake for about 20 minutes. This cake is fragile, so take care when handling it. Let cool for 10–15 minutes, then run a knife around the edge to loosen it from the pan. Cool completely. Turn out very carefully on to a serving plate. The base will become the top. Remove the paper.

To make the ganache, melt the chocolate, cream and butter in a heatproof bowl set over very gently simmering water (make sure the bottom of the bowl does not touch the water). Stir well and remove from the heat. Cool a little until it thickens, then pour and spread it over the cake with a metal icing spatula. Stud the surface with the raspberries.

SERVES 8

FOR THE CAKE
½ cup (2 ounces) skinned
   hazelnuts
5½ ounces bittersweet chocolate
   (70% cacao), chopped
scant ½ cup organic sugar
6 tablespoons unsalted butter,
   cubed, plus more for the pan
3 large eggs, separated

FOR THE GANACHE
3½ ounces bittersweet chocolate
   (70% cacao), chopped
3 tablespoons heavy cream
2 tablespoons unsalted butter
12-14 ounces fresh raspberries

victoria sponge cake

This 1-bowl method takes no time at all to whip up, is completely fail-safe and gives a delicious buttery cake.

Preheat the oven to 350°F.

You can choose to cook this cake either in one or two 8 x 1 ½" round cake pans. Butter the pan or pans. Line the bottoms with parchment paper. If you use just 1 pan, line the sides with a 3"-high collar of parchment paper as well, to allow for the rise.

For this batter, I use an electric mixer and beater attachment, but use a food processor, or a bowl and an electric whisk, if you wish.

Sift the flour and baking powder into the bowl, then add the butter (cut into tablespoons), the eggs, sugar, and vanilla. Beat together until thoroughly blended, about 2 minutes on high speed. Scrape the batter into the pan or pans and smooth the top.

Bake for 20–25 minutes if you are using two pans, or 30–35 minutes for 1 pan, until the cake springs back to the touch or a wooden toothpick inserted into the center comes out clean.

Remove from the oven and let cool for a couple of minutes. Run a knife around the rim to loosen the cake from the pan and turn out on to a wire rack. Peel off the paper and cool completely.

Lightly whip the cream until just thickened into soft peaks. If you have baked the cake in 1 pan, split horizontally with a serrated knife. Fill with jam and cream and sandwich together, so the cream forms the upper layer. If you have baked the cake in 2 pans, be sure to sandwich the flat bases together. Sift confectioners' sugar on top.

SERVES 8

FOR THE CAKE
1¼ cups self-rising flour
1 teaspoon baking powder
¾ cup unsalted butter, softened, plus more for the pan
3 large eggs, lightly beaten
¾ cup plus 2 tablespoons organic sugar
1 teaspoon vanilla extract

FOR THE FILLING
½ cup heavy cream
¼ cup raspberry or strawberry jam
confectioners' sugar, for garnish

TO DECORATE see: Gala Cake, page 92; Pink Iced Heart, page 117; Fresh Petal Confetti Cake, page 122; Butterfly Cakes, page 153; Garland Cakes, page 154; Rosebud Cupcakes, page 157; Fondant Petits Fours, page 163; Fancy Hats, page 173

battenberg cake

This two-toned cake is said to have been created for the marriage of Queen Victoria's granddaughter to Prince Louis of Battenberg in 1884. Each square represents one of the four Battenberg princes: Louis, Alexander, Henry and Francis Joseph. It is exceptionally pretty and worth making, even if the occasion isn't a royal wedding!

Preheat the oven to 350°F. Lightly butter an 8" square baking pan and line the bottom with parchment paper. Also cut out a rectangle of parchment paper, as long and deep as the pan, to act as a divider lengthways between the 2 colors of batter.

In the bowl of an electric mixer, or in a large bowl with a hand mixer, first sift together the flour and baking powder. Add the butter (cut into tablespoons), the sugar, eggs, and vanilla. Beat until smooth, adding a little milk to loosen the batter if it seems too stiff. Place the divider down the center of the pan.

Carefully spread half the batter in 1 side of the pan. Tint the remaining batter pink - it's much better to do this not too exuberantly, so take care! - and stir until blended. As neatly as possible, spread the pink batter in the other side of the pan.

Bake for about 30–35 minutes, or until a wooden toothpick inserted into the center comes out clean and the cake springs back to the touch. Remove from the oven, and cool in the pan for a few minutes. Turn out on to a wire rack. Remove the paper and cool completely. Slice each color lengthwise into 2 equal blocks, then trim off all the rough edges.

Warm the jam in a small pan, then rub it through a sieve. Use the jam to glue the strips of cake together lengthwise, so the natural and pink colors form opposite quadrants.

On a work surface dusted with confectioners' sugar, roll out the marzipan into a rectangle the length of the cake and wide enough to wrap around all 4 sides. Trim it to size. Brush the remaining jam all over the cake and wrap the marzipan around the cake. Seal the seam by gently pressing it together, then turn so this seam is hidden on the bottom. Trim the ends with a sharp knife, then score a criss-cross on the top surface.

SERVES 8

1¼ cups self-rising flour
½ teaspoon baking powder
¾ cup unsalted butter, softened, plus more for the pan
¾ cup plus 2 tablespoons superfine sugar
3 large eggs, lightly beaten
1 teaspoon vanilla extract
1 to 2 tablespoons milk, if needed
a little pink (or red) food coloring
¼ cup apricot jam
confectioners' sugar, for garnish
9 ounces store-bought yellow marzipan, tinted yellow or left natural, as desired

sticky ginger cake

A wonderful cake that should be left alone for a couple of days before eating…that's the hardest part! It's also delicious with my Salted Caramel Buttercream (see page 64, use half the quantity).

Preheat the oven to 350°F. Butter an 8 x 3" deep cake pan and line with parchment paper.

Place the butter, sugar, milk, molasses, and syrup into a saucepan and very gently melt together. Do not boil or it will curdle. Remove from the heat and cool a little.

In a large bowl, sift together the flour, ginger, and baking soda. Add the butter mixture and fold together with a large spoon. Add the eggs, mix well and pour the batter into the pan. Rap a couple of times on a work surface to release any bubbles. Bake for 40–50 minutes until firm to the touch and a wooden toothpick inserted into the center comes out clean.

Cool in the pan for about 15 minutes. Turn out on to a rack, remove the paper and cool completely. Wrap the cake in parchment paper and then in aluminum foil and let stand at room temperature for a couple of days. This will make it very moist with a slightly sticky surface.

When ready to serve, make the lime buttercream. Place the confectioners' sugar and butter in the bowl of an electric mixer (or use a bowl and a hand mixer) and beat for a good 5 minutes. Add the lime zest and slowly pour in the juice, still beating. Spread the buttercream over the cake. Scatter with the cookies, if using.

SERVES 10

FOR THE CAKE
9 tablespoons unsalted butter, plus more for the pan
½ cup plus 1 tablespoon packed brown sugar
½ cup milk
⅓ cup plus 1 tablespoon molasses
⅓ cup golden syrup
1½ cups all-purpose flour
1 tablespoon ground ginger
½ teaspoon baking soda
2 large eggs, lightly beaten
3 thin, crisp cookies, lightly crushed (optional)

FOR THE LIME BUTTERCREAM
1¼ cups confectioners' sugar, sifted
7 tablespoons unsalted butter, softened
finely grated zest and juice of ½ large lime

TO DECORATE see: Mosaic Cake, page 90

very lemony crunch cake

This moist cake is doused in lemon syrup to give it a
wonderfully crunchy top.

Preheat the oven to 350°F.

Lightly butter a 7" springform pan and line the bottom and sides with
parchment paper.

Sift the flour and salt into a bowl and set aside. Melt the butter in a
small saucepan and set aside to cool slightly. Using an electric mixer
on high speed, beat the eggs and sugar together until very light and
fluffy (this may take 5 minutes). Blend in the melted butter; then very
gently fold in the flour mixture and lemon zest. Finally, slowly fold in
the lemon juice.

Pour and spread the batter into the pan. Bake for 30–35 minutes
or until the cake springs back to the touch, or a wooden toothpick
inserted into the center comes out clean.

Meanwhile, make the crunchy topping by simply mixing the sugar
and lemon juice together in a small bowl. As soon as the cake comes
from the oven, pierce tiny holes all over it with a wooden toothpick.
Pour the lemon syrup evenly all over the surface. Let cool completely
in the pan. Remove the side of the pan and the side papers. Cover a
wire rack with a silicone baking mat or parchment paper. Invert the
cake on to the rack and immediately remove the bottom paper. Invert
again, right side up.

SERVES 6

FOR THE CAKE
1¼ cups self-rising flour
a pinch of salt
¾ cup unsalted butter, softened,
    plus more for the pan
2 large eggs, lightly beaten
¾ cup plus 2 tablespoons organic
    sugar
finely grated zest and juice of 1
    large organic lemon

FOR THE TOPPING
½ cup granulated sugar
juice of 1 large organic lemon

TO DECORATE see: Pansy Wreath, page 104; Fairy Tale Garden Cakes, page 178;
    Tiny Fairy Cakes, page 181

orange drizzle cake

This is a very versatile recipe; try it with lemon zest and juice, too. It makes a firmer cake than the Very Lemony Crunch Cake (page 31), so is an excellent base for decorating.

Preheat the oven to 350°F.

Butter an 8" springform pan, then line the bottom with parchment paper.

Cream the butter, sugar, and zest until very pale, light and fluffy (it will take at least 5 minutes in an electric mixer on high speed). Add the eggs gradually, beating between each addition, along with 1 tablespoon of the flour to prevent curdling. Fold in the remaining flour, then slowly mix in the orange juice.

Pour the mixture into the pan. Bake for 40–45 minutes until the cake springs back to the touch, or a wooden toothpick inserted into center comes out clean. Remove from the oven, leave for 1 minute, and let cool. Turn out on to a wire rack and remove the paper. Cool completely.

To make the icing, sift the confectioners' sugar into a bowl. Slowly stir in the orange juice and orange flower water, until the mixture coats the back of a spoon. Pour and spread the icing over the cake, letting it drizzle down the sides. Let stand until the icing sets, about 1 hour.

SERVES 8

FOR THE CAKE
1 cup unsalted butter, softened, plus more for the pan
1¼ cups organic sugar
finely grated zest of 2 large organic oranges, plus ¼ cup fresh orange juice
4 large eggs, lightly beaten
1¾ cups self-rising flour, sifted

FOR THE ICING
1¾ cups confectioners' sugar
3 to 4 tablespoons fresh orange juice
a few drops of orange flower water

TO DECORATE see: Maypole, page 112; Tiered Marie Antoinette's Cake, page 146; Crystallized Flower Cupcakes, page 158; Ice-cream Cones, page 160

genoise

This classic French cake, the cornerstone of numerous *gateaux*, is very light. It is a little trickier than most of my other cakes, but provided the recipe is followed closely it should be as light as a feather. I have used no butter (except for the pan) so it does not keep well; eat it on the day it is made. If you like, try sprinkling a couple of spoonfuls of liqueur or syrup over the cooled cake. Use whatever you have, maybe Cointreau or cassis.

Preheat the oven to 350°F. Butter a 9" springform pan and line the bottom and sides with parchment paper.

Sift the flour and salt together into a bowl twice for extra fineness and lightness. Warm the whisk and bowl of a standing mixer by submerging both in hot water, then drying thoroughly.

Crack the eggs into the bowl, beat a little with a fork, then add the sugar. Start the mixer slowly, then turn up the speed to its highest. You will see the mixture increasing in volume quite dramatically and becoming lighter and paler until it looks like a mousse. This may well take 5 minutes on high speed. (If you use a hand mixer, allow an extra minute or two.) It is crucial to stop at the right point, which is when you can drizzle a trail of mixture with the whisk which sits on the top of the rest of the batter for a few seconds; this is called the ribbon stage.

In 3 or 4 batches, fold in the flour as lightly as possible with a rubber spatula, adding the vanilla as well. Inevitably, the mixture will start to lose the volume that you want to keep so, for the lightest result, do this as gently as you can.

Bake for 20–25 minutes, until the top springs back when lightly pressed with a finger and a wooden toothpick inserted into the center comes out clean. Turn out on to a wire rack covered with a piece of parchment paper to keep the cake from sticking. Remove the paper. Let cool completely.

Whip the cream until soft peaks form, adding the confectioners' sugar to taste, then the vanilla. Slice the cake in half horizontally. Spread the bottom with the cream and top with the fruits. Sandwich with the top half, then sift confectioners' sugar over the top.

TO DECORATE see: Blackberry and Geranium Genoise, page 87

SERVES 8

FOR THE CAKE
a little softened butter for the pan
¾ cup plus 2 tablespoons all-purpose flour
a pinch of salt
4 large eggs
⅔ cup organic sugar
1 teaspoon vanilla extract

FOR THE FILLING
½ cup heavy cream
2 tablespoons confectioners' sugar, plus more for garnish
1 teaspoon vanilla extract
2 cups fruit of your choice: sliced peaches or nectarines, strawberries, blueberries, or raspberries

coffee and hazelnut cake

You can use drip, espresso, or instant coffee...whatever you prefer and have in the cupboard. And you can choose which nuts you would like; you may want the more classic combination of coffee with walnut or pecan, or try almonds or even macadamias.

Preheat the oven to 350°F.

Lightly butter two 8 x 2" round cake pans, then line the bottoms with parchment paper.

Spread the hazelnuts on a baking sheet. Bake for 5-10 minutes until lightly toasted, shaking the sheet once and watching carefully to make sure they don't burn. Let cool. Finely chop 2/3 cup of the hazelnuts and set aside for the cake. Coarsely chop the remaining hazelnuts and reserve for the garnish.

Sift together the flour and baking powder into a bowl and set aside. In an electric mixer, or in a large bowl with a hand mixer, cream together the butter and sugar for about 5 minutes until very light and fluffy. Add the eggs very slowly, with the mixer running, adding 1 tablespoon of the flour during the process to prevent curdling. Finally, using a large rubber spatula, fold in the remaining flour, the finely chopped hazelnuts, milk, and coffee until well blended.

Spread the batter evenly between the pans. Bake for 25–30 minutes until the cakes spring back to the touch, or a wooden toothpick inserted into the center comes out clean. Remove from the oven and let cool slightly in the pans. Turn out on to wire racks. Remove the papers and cool completely.

Meanwhile, make the buttercream. Cream the butter and sugar together for at least 5 minutes until really light and airy, then add the coffee. Mix well. Spread half the coffee buttercream on to the base of one cake, lay the other cake on top (flat bottoms together) and finish with the remaining buttercream. Sprinkle the coarsely chopped hazelnuts on top.

TO DECORATE see: Giant Cupcake, page 101

SERVES 8

FOR THE CAKE
1 cup (4 ounces) skinned
  hazelnuts
1½ cups self-rising flour
1 teaspoon baking powder
1 cup unsalted butter, softened,
  plus more for the pan
2/3 cup packed brown sugar
4 large eggs, lightly beaten
2 tablespoons milk
2 tablespoons very strong brewed
  coffee

FOR THE BUTTERCREAM
7 tablespoons unsalted butter,
  softened
1¾ cups confectioners' sugar
2 tablespoons very strong brewed
  coffee, cooled

pistachio and orange blossom cake

I love the combination of delicate flavors here, and the creamy mascarpone topping acts as a perfect contrast.

Preheat the oven to 350°F. Lightly butter an 8" springform pan, and line with parchment paper.

Spread the pistachios on to a baking sheet. Bake for about 5 minutes, shaking once and watching all the time to make sure they don't burn. Let cool. Grind finely in a food processor.

In a large bowl, sift together the flour, baking powder, and salt. Then, in an electric mixer, cream together the butter, sugar and zest until very light and fluffy – expect it to take about 5 minutes – and slowly add the eggs, adding 1 tablespoon of the flour mixture as you do so to prevent curdling. Fold in the almonds and pistachios, the remaining flour and then the orange flower water.

Spread the batter into the pan. Bake for about 40 minutes, or until a wooden toothpick inserted into the center comes out clean.

Meanwhile, make the syrup: combine the orange juice, sugar, and orange flower water in a small saucepan and bring to a rolling boil. Cook until reduced to about 1/4 cup.

As soon as the cake comes from the oven, pierce it all over with a wooden toothpick and evenly drizzle with the syrup. Let cool completely in the pan.

Unmold the cake on to a serving platter, so the flat bottom now forms the top. Remove the paper. Beat together all the ingredients for the mascarpone topping, and spread it on with a spatula.

SERVES 8

FOR THE CAKE
scant 1 cup (3 1/2 ounces) shelled
    unsalted pistachios
1/2 cup self-rising flour
1 teaspoon baking powder
pinch of salt
3/4 cup unsalted butter, softened,
    plus more for the pan
1 cup organic sugar
finely grated zest of 1 organic
    orange
4 large eggs, lightly beaten
2/3 cup almond flour
2 teaspoons orange flower water

FOR THE SYRUP
juice of 1 organic orange
1/4 cup organic sugar
1 tablespoon orange flower water

FOR THE TOPPING
9 ounces mascarpone
finely grated zest of 1 organic
    orange
2 tablespoons superfine sugar
1 teaspoon orange flower water
1/2 teaspoon vanilla extract

TO DECORATE see: Rose Garden, page 109

star anise, almond, and clementine cake

The exotic flavor of star anise - a beautiful flower-shaped spice - permeates this lovely, moist cake. You can use lemongrass instead if you prefer for the syrup: split and slightly crush 2 stalks to bring out the flavor. You need to make the syrup a few hours in advance or, even better, the day before to allow the flavors to develop. Try this recipe with tangerines or oranges if clementines are out of season.

A few hours before, or the day before, you bake the cake, make the syrup. Gently boil together the clementine juice, sugar, and star anise until it reduces by half. Cover and let infuse at room temperature to develop flavor.

Preheat the oven to 350°F.

Butter an 8" springform pan, then line the bottom and sides with parchment paper.

Cream the butter, sugar, and zest together in a bowl with an electric mixer on high speed, until very light and fluffy (this will take a good 5 minutes). Add the eggs very slowly. With a large metal spoon, fold in the almond flour, all-purpose flour and baking powder.

Pour the batter into the cake pan and level the surface. Bake for 45–50 minutes or until a wooden toothpick inserted into the center comes out clean.

Let the cake cool in the pan for 5 minutes. Remove the sides of the pan. Invert the pan on to a plate and remove the pan bottom and paper. Place a wire rack over the cake and invert. Pierce holes all over the surface. Drizzle evenly with the syrup and garnish with the star anise. Cool completely.

SERVES 8

FOR THE SYRUP
1/3 cup fresh clementine juice
   (about 2 fruits)
1/4 cup packed brown sugar
5–6 star anise

FOR THE CAKE
1 cup plus 2 tablespoons unsalted
   butter, softened, plus more for
   the pan
1 cup plus 2 tablespoons organic
   sugar
finely grated zest of 4
   clementines
4 large eggs, lightly beaten
2 1/4 cups almond flour
1/2 cup all-purpose flour, sifted
1 teaspoon baking powder

TO DECORATE see: Eastern Fantasy, page 89

carrot-pecan cake with maple syrup and orange buttercream

This moist cake rose to prominence in the 1970s and remains hugely popular. The flavors in the buttercream are a wonderful complement.

Preheat the oven to 325°F.

Oil a 9" springform pan and line the bottom with parchment paper.

Spread the pecans on to a baking sheet. Bake for 5–10 minutes, shaking once and watching carefully so they don't burn. Cool completely. Chop the pecans.

Sift together the flour, cinnamon, nutmeg, baking soda, baking powder, and salt into a large bowl. With an electric mixer, slowly beat together the oil and sugar for a minute or so until smooth. Gradually add the eggs, beating well after each addition. Using a large spoon, gently fold in the carrots, ²⁄₃ cup of the pecans, coconut, and orange zest. Fold in the flour mixture.

Spread the batter into the pan. Bake for 1 hour, or until a wooden toothpick inserted into the center comes out clean. Cool in the pan for a few minutes, then turn out on to a wire rack. Remove the paper and cool completely.

Meanwhile, make the buttercream. Beat the butter, confectioners' sugar, and maple syrup with an electric mixer on high speed until really light and fluffy (this could take 5 minutes). In another bowl, beat the cream cheese until smooth, then mix it into the butter mixture. Finally, mix in enough of the orange juice to make a spreadable buttercream. Spread over the top of the cake and sprinkle with the remaining ¹⁄₃ cup pecans.

SERVES 10

FOR THE CAKE
1 cup (4 ounces) pecans
1¹⁄₃ cups self-rising flour
2 teaspoons cinnamon
1 teaspoon freshly grated nutmeg
½ teaspoon baking soda
½ teaspoon baking powder
pinch of salt
²⁄₃ cup sunflower oil, plus more for the pan
¾ cup packed brown sugar
3 large eggs, lightly beaten
1²⁄₃ cups (9 ounces) shredded carrots
½ cup unsweetened desiccated coconut
finely grated zest of 1 organic orange

FOR THE BUTTERCREAM
6 tablespoons unsalted butter, softened
½ cup confectioners' sugar, sifted
2 tablespoons maple syrup
5½ ounces cream cheese, softened
juice of 1 organic orange

TO DECORATE see: Daisy and Sunflower Cupcakes, page 169; Mini Tiered Cakes, page 175

tropical fruit cake

This gingery, rum-laced cake is a twist on the classic fruit cake. When I was dreaming this up, I thought of all the flavors of exotic sun-soaked holidays and put those in instead of the more usual fruits and nuts. You'll need to start this cake the day before to let the fruits soak up the rum.

The day before, rinse the cherries for the cake, then dry on paper towels and chop. Place the cherries, apricots, dates, ginger, raisins, and currants in a large bowl and pour over the rum, lime zest and lime juice. Stir well, cover with plastic wrap and let stand overnight.

The next day, preheat the oven to 275°F. Lightly butter an 8 x 3" square baking pan and line with parchment paper. Wrap the outside of the tin with a collar of brown paper (or even newspaper works fine) and tie with string. (Do this every time you are baking fruit cakes that need long cooking, to protect the outsides from scorching in the pan.)

Spread the pistachios and pecans on a baking tray. Bake for 10 minutes. Cool, chop, and set aside. Sift the flour, pie spice, ground ginger and salt together. In the bowl of an electric mixer, cream together the butter and sugar until really light and fluffy (this will take at least 5 minutes). Add the almond flour. Very gradually stir in the eggs, mixing well after each addition. Stir in the flour mixture and molasses. Gently fold in all the nuts and the fruits with their delicious rummy liquid.

Spread the mixture in the pan. To decorate, arrange the cherries, pecans, and pistachios on top. Bake on an oven rack in the lower third of the oven for about 2½–3 hours or until a wooden toothpick inserted into the center comes out clean. If it browns too much before it is fully cooked, make a square of foil a bit larger than the cake, pierce a hole in the center and open it up, then place it over the cake

Let cool in the pan. Pierce it all over with a wooden toothpick and sprinkle with the extra rum. Remove the cake from the pan and remove the paper. Wrap in fresh parchment paper, then aluminum foil, and let mature for a week - even a month - though it will still taste delicious if you serve it immediately.

TO DECORATE see: Glacé Fruit and Nut Cake, page 133; Christmas Gifts, page 182

MAKES 25 SLICES

1 cup candied cherries
1 cup chopped dried apricots
1 cup chopped dates
1 cup chopped crystallized ginger
1 cup golden raisins
1 cup dried currants
½ cup dark rum (plus a couple of tablespoons more to feed the cake)
finely grated zest and juice of 2 limes
1 cup (4 ounces) shelled unsalted pistachios
1 cup (4 ounces) pecans
1 cup self-rising flour
1 teaspoon apple pie spice
1 tablespoon ground ginger
1 teaspoon salt
1⅓ cups unsalted butter, softened, plus more for the pan
¾ cup packed dark brown sugar
1½ cups almond flour
5 large eggs, lightly beaten
2 tablespoons molasses

TO DECORATE
12 candied cherries
18 pecans
24 shelled unsalted pistachios

rich tamarind fruit cake

I started my business using this particularly moist,
dark recipe as a Christmas cake, producing hundreds of
miniatures cooked in baked bean cans from my kitchen table
(see page 182 for more cakes cooked in cans). It has been
tweaked by adding tamarind, my husband's bright idea!
Make it up to 3 months in advance, or at least a week before
you want it, to let it mature and absorb the brandy.

The day before, rinse the cherries, then dry them well with paper
towels and cut each in half. Place the golden and dark raisins, mixed
peel, ginger, currants, cherries, molasses, marmalade, tamarind
paste, zests and spice into a large bowl. Pour in 6 tablespoons of the
brandy, stir well, cover with plastic wrap and let stand overnight.

The next day, preheat the oven to 275°F. Lightly butter a 9"
springform pan and line the bottom and sides with parchment paper.
Wrap the outside of the pan with brown paper and tie with string, to
protect the cake from scorching in the oven.

Spread the nuts on a baking sheet. Bake for 10 minutes in the oven,
shaking once. Cool slightly, chop coarsely and set aside.

Sift the flour and salt into a bowl. In an electric mixer on high speed,
beat the butter and sugar for at least 5 minutes until it turns pale and
fluffy. Add the ground almonds, then very gradually the eggs, mixing
well between each addition. Fold in the flour with a large metal spoon
and then the soaked fruits (and any liquid) and nuts.

Spread the batter into the pan. Bake on an oven rack in the lower third
of the oven for about 2½–3 hours. If a wooden toothpick inserted
into the center comes out clean, it is ready. If it browns too much
before it is fully cooked, make a circle of foil a bit larger than the cake,
pierce a hole in the center and open it up, then place it over the pan.

Let cool in the pan. Pierce all over with a wooden toothpick and
evenly sprinkle over the remaining 3 tablespoons brandy. Remove
from the pan and discard the paper. Wrap in fresh parchment paper,
then aluminum foil, and let stand for a week or up to 3 months.
Unwrap and sprinkle with with 1 tablespoon more brandy every other
week, if you like, for extra succulence and booziness!

TO DECORATE see: Christmas Trees, page 130; Gingerbread Man Cake,
page 137; Vintage Glamour Wedding Cake, page 140

MAKES 25–30 SLICES

- 1½ cups candied cherries
- 2 cups golden raisins
- 2 cups dark raisins, preferably
  Thompson
- 1¼ cups mixed candied citrus peel
- ⅔ cup chopped crystallized ginger
- ½ cup dried currants
- 3 tablespoons molasses
- 3 tablespoons bitter orange
  marmalade
- 1 teaspoon tamarind concentrate
- finely grated zest of 1 organic
  orange
- finely grated zest of 1 organic
  lemon
- 1 heaped tablespoon apple pie spice
- 6 tablespoons brandy, plus 3
  tablespoons to feed the cake
- 1 cup (4 ounces) walnuts
- ⅓ cup (1½ ounces) blanched
  almonds
- 1¼ cups self-rising flour
- 1 teaspoon salt
- 1 cup plus 2 tablespoons unsalted
  butter, softened, plus more for
  the pan
- 1 cup plus 2 tablespoons packed
  brown sugar
- 1½ cups almond flour
- 5 large eggs, lightly beaten

whisky, date, and walnut cake

Whisky and shortbread may be Scotland's greatest culinary exports and, due to my Scottish roots, both have found their way into this book. If you can sneak in a splash of malt whisky, it will make it extra special. You'll need to start the cake the day before, to plump up the fruits in whisky.

The day before, place the cherries and dates in a bowl and pour in the whisky. Mix well, cover with plastic wrap and let stand overnight.

Preheat the oven to 275°F. Butter a large (12^1/$_2$ x 4^1/$_2$") loaf pan, or an 8" springform pan, or an 8" square baking pan, and line the bottom and sides with parchment paper. Wrap the pan with a collar of brown paper tied with string.

Roast the walnut pieces on a baking sheet in the oven for 10 minutes, then cool and coarsely chop them. Using an electric mixer on high speed, cream together the butter, sugar, and zests for a good 5 minutes until light and fluffy. Next, add the almond flour, then gradually beat in the eggs, mixing thoroughly between each addition. Add the molasses, then fold in the flour. Finally, very gently fold in the nuts, cherries, and dates, along with any whisky that has not been absorbed. Add enough milk to make a smooth batter that drops easily from the spoon.

Spread the batter evenly into the pan, and decorate with the 5 walnut halves. Bake for about 1^1/$_2$ hours, or until a wooden toothpick inserted into the center comes out clean.

Let the cake cool in the pan. Pierce with a wooden toothpick and drizzle with the extra whisky. Remove the cake from the pan and discard the paper. Wrap the cake in fresh parchment paper, then in aluminum foil, and store for up to a month.

MAKES 12 SLICES

^{3}/$_4$ cup candied cherries, halved

1 cup pitted and quartered dates

^{1}/$_3$ cup Scotch whisky (plus a couple of tablespoons more to feed the cake)

1^3/$_4$ cups walnut pieces, plus 5 walnut halves for decoration

11 tablespoons unsalted butter, softened, plus more for the pan

^{3}/$_4$ cup packed brown sugar

finely grated zest of 1 organic orange

finely grated zest of 1 organic lemon

2 tablespoons almond flour

3 large eggs, lightly beaten

1 tablespoon molasses

1^1/$_2$ cups self-rising flour, sifted

3 tablespoons milk, as needed

TO DECORATE see: Marzipan Criss-Cross, page 138

cherry and marzipan cake

Use the best candied cherries you can find. If you can get candied sour cherries (I used some from Poland), then do try them - they elevate this recipe into something very special - though it does still taste great with normal candied cherries. The layer of marzipan melts into the cake.

Preheat the oven to 350°F. Butter a 12¹/₂ x 4¹/₂ x 2¹/₂" loaf pan, or a 9" round cake pan, and line the base with parchment paper.

Rinse and completely dry the cherries on kitchen towel. Sift the flour and baking powder into a bowl and set aside. Roll out the marzipan between 2 sheets of plastic wrap into a very thin rectangle or circle, slightly smaller than the pan, and set aside.

Cream the butter, organic sugar and zest together in an electric mixer on full speed until very pale, light and fluffy (this will take about 5 minutes).

Beat in the eggs a little at a time, adding 1 tablespoon flour during the process to stop the mixture from curdling. Fold in the almond flour, the sifted flour mixture, and the lemon juice until well blended, then spoon half the cake mixture into the pan. Place half the cherries over the batter in a shape echoing that of the pan, towards the middle. This will support the marzipan. Lay on the marzipan, then add the remaining cherries, again in a shape echoing the pan, but this time towards the outer edge. Pour in the remaining batter and level with a spatula. Sprinkle over the demerara sugar. Bake for 50–60 minutes, or until a wooden toothpick comes out clean and the center of the cake springs back to the touch.

Cool the cake in the pan for 15–20 minutes. Turn out on to a wire rack and remove the paper. Cool completely. Don't worry if it sinks a bit in the middle; it's due to the weight of the marzipan and cherries. If decorating, simply invert it so the flat bottom forms the top.

SERVES 8

1 cup unsalted butter, softened, plus more for the pan
1¹/₂ cups imported candied cherries
1¹/₂ cups self-rising flour
¹/₂ teaspoon baking powder
5 ounces marzipan (see page 138), or use store-bought
³/₄ cup plus 2 tablespoons organic sugar
finely grated zest of 1 organic lemon, plus 2 tablespoons lemon juice
4 large eggs, lightly beaten
1 cup plus 2 tablespoons almond flour
2 tablespoons demerara sugar

TO DECORATE see: Summer Cherries, page 95; Ribbon Roses, page 120; Fluttering Butterflies, page 125

vegan fruit cake

For vegans, those with allergies to dairy products or indeed anyone wanting a speedy, delicious fruit cake, this is for you. It contains neither eggs nor butter, has very little added sugar, is packed with moist fruit and roasted nuts, then laced with rum. The recipe was originally devised for Sir Paul McCartney at Christmas.

Preheat the oven to 275°F.

Oil a 9" springform pan and line the bottom and sides with parchment paper. Wrap the outside of the pan with brown paper and tie it securely with string.

Chop all the nuts and roast in the oven for 10–15 minutes, watching carefully to make sure they don't burn. Place the dried fruits, oil, orange juice and brown sugar in a heavy-bottomed saucepan, add 1 cup water, bring to a boil and simmer over low heat for 5 minutes. Let cool. Fold in all the other ingredients. Transfer the batter to the prepared pan. Bake for 2½ hours, or until a wooden toothpick inserted into the center comes out clean. If the cake browns too much before it is fully baked, make a circle of aluminum foil a bit larger than the cake, break a large hole in the center and place it over the cake to protect the sides from burning.

Let cool in the pan. Turn out on to a wire rack and remove the paper. Pierce all over with a wooden toothpickand sprinkle the remaining 3 tablespoons rum over the cake.

Wrap in fresh parchment paper, then in aluminum foil, and store for up to 6 weeks.

TO DECORATE see: Fruit-and-Nut Cupcakes, page 186

SERVES 15 SLICES

½ cup sunflower oil, plus more for the pan
½ cup (2 ounces) whole blanched almonds
½ cup (2 ounces) walnut pieces
2 cups dark raisins (preferably Thompson)
1⅔ cups golden raisins
¾ cup dried currants
½ cup fresh orange juice
6 tablespoons packed brown sugar
2⅔ cups self-rising flour, sifted
3 tablespoons rum or brandy, plus 3 tablespoons more to feed the cake
1 tablespoon molasses
1 teaspoon apple pie spice
finely grated zest of 1 organic lemon
finely grated zest of 1 organic orange
¼ teaspoon salt

exotic fruit chewy pavlova

This is a crisp meringue with a soft marshmallowy center, lavishly topped with a tangy lemon and passion fruit cream and winter fruits. Here we photographed a 9" single disk, which would need exactly half the ingredients given and serve six. If you want to make this smaller meringue, be generous with the fruits and use about 3 cups total. Read my tips on perfect meringues (see page 71) before you begin.

Line 2 baking sheets with parchment paper. Preheat the oven to 400°F. Draw 3 circles on parchment paper, the first 4" in diameter, another 7" and the last 10" (use plates, saucers, or cans as a guide).

Stir together the cornstarch and vinegar in a small bowl until well blended. In a large, clean bowl, whisk the egg whites and salt with an electric mixer until they form soft peaks. Add the superfine sugar 1 tablespoon at a time, and the cornstarch mixture. The meringue should be thick, shiny, and marshmallowy.

Using a spatula, spread the mixture into the 3 circles. Keep the disks reasonably flat. Put them in the oven and immediately reduce the temperature to 175°F. Bake for $1^3/_4 - 2$ hours. They should be crispy and dry on the outside and may be a bit cracked, which is fine. Give them a bit longer in the oven if necessary, but they may start to color a little; try to keep them as white as possible. Turn the oven off, leave the door slightly ajar and let cool completely in the oven.

Whip the cream until soft peaks form, then fold in the confectioners' sugar to taste and the vanilla. Fold in half the lemon curd. Cut open the passion fruit and scoop out the pulp. Peel and pit the mango and chop. Peel the pineapple and chop into bite-sized pieces. Deseed the pomegranate. Place the 10" meringue on a serving plate. Spread with some cream, then a layer of fruit, reserving a few pomegranate seeds. Add more cream, then place on the 7" meringue. Repeat with the remaining cream and fruits and top with the 4" meringue. Sprinkle with the reserved pomegranate. Sift a generous amount of confectioners' sugar on top, and a scattering of edible glitter, if you wish.

SERVES 12

FOR THE MERINGUE
4 teaspoons cornstarch
4 teaspoons white wine vinegar
8 large egg whites, at room
  temperature
pinch of salt
$2^2/_3$ cups superfine sugar

FOR THE FILLING
2 cups heavy cream
4 tablespoons confectioners'
  sugar, plus more for garnish
2 teaspoons vanilla extract or
  seeds from 1 vanilla bean
6 tablespoons store-bought lemon
  curd
3 ripe, crinkly passion fruits
5 cups mixed exotic fruits of
  your choice (I used mangoes,
  pineapple, and pomegranate)
clear edible glitter (optional)

TO DECORATE see: Summer Berry Rose-scented Meringue, page 114

surprise icebox cake

This recipe has two huge advantages: not only will you become unbelievably popular overnight with your children (it disappeared, mysteriously, very quickly in our household), it's also a snap to make. The surprise is that, hidden inside, are your kids' favorite candies. Of course, you could always make it healthier by using chopped dried fruits and nuts instead, but you might not be so popular!

You will need a $9^1/_2$ x $4^1/_2$" loaf pan, or an 8" square baking pan. Butter the pan and line it with plastic wrap, allowing a generous excess to overhang the edges.

Crush the cookies into small pieces by placing them in a plastic bag and smashing with a rolling pin. In a small saucepan, very gently melt together the chocolate, butter, sugar, syrup, and cocoa. Remove from the heat and cool until tepid. Add the cookies and stir in the chocolates and candies. Mix well and spoon into the pan. Cover the top with the excess plastic wrap and refrigerate for a few hours to set. Remove the cake from the pan by pulling on the plastic wrap and easing it out with a knife. Turn it out on to a wire rack set over a rimmed baking sheet.

For the topping, place a small heatproof bowl over a saucepan of gently simmering water, making sure the bottom of the bowl does not touch the water. Add the chocolate to the bowl and heat until it melts, stirring only very occasionally, then pour over the cake. Let the chocolate set. Transfer to a serving platter. Store in the refrigerator – preferably hidden! – until you serve it. It will cut much more easily if it is not kept for too long at room temperature.

SERVES 12

FOR THE CAKE
6 ounces shortbread cookies
2 ounces semisweet chocolate (50% cacao), chopped
8 tablespoons unsalted butter, cubed, plus more for the pan
$1/_2$ cup organic sugar
2 tablespoons golden syrup
1 tablespoon cocoa powder
6 ounces assorted candies and chocolates (I used mini marshmallows, crushed honeycomb chocolate bars, malted chocolate balls, and caramel chocolates)

FOR THE TOPPING
3-4 ounces semisweet chocolate (50% cacao), chopped

TO DECORATE see: Penguin Cake, page 134; Melting Snowmen, page 185

dark chocolate mousse cake

A surprisingly light chocolate mousse on a base of Chocolate Tiffin (page 68). This is really simple, but the trick is that both the cream and chocolate need to be at room temperature. Keep the cake in the refrigerator until shortly before serving.

Butter a 9" springform pan, ensuring the rim is facing down so it is easy to remove the cake later. Fill the base with the freshly prepared Chocolate Tiffin mixture, levelling it evenly by pressing with the back of a teaspoon. Refrigerate for a few hours until set.

Melt the chocolate in a good-sized heatproof bowl set over a pan of barely simmering water (make sure the bottom of the bowl does not touch the water), then add the kirsch. Cool until the mixture is tepid, but fluid. In a large bowl, whisk the cream until slightly thickened and the whisk leaves a trail.

Now, very gently whisk half the whipped cream into the chocolate. Fold in the remaining cream with a rubber spatula, until thoroughly blended and smooth. Be gentle. Pour into the pan and chill overnight in the refrigerator.

When ready to serve, remove from the refrigerator. Dip a knife into hot water before running it all around the edge. Remove the sides of the pan. Lift on to a serving plate or cake stand. You should be able to loosen the tiffin from the pan base by running a metal icing spatula between them. Finish with a dusting of cocoa powder, if you wish. This cake can't be left a long time at room temperature, so serve shortly after it comes out of the refrigerator.

SERVES 12

a little softened butter, for the pan
1 recipe Chocolate Tiffin, without gold leaf, (page 68), unchilled
10½ ounces semisweet or bittersweet chocolate (50–70% cacao), chopped
1 tablespoon kirsch or Cointreau
1¾ cups heavy cream
1 tablespoon cocoa powder, for garnish (optional)

TO DECORATE see: Easter Chocolate Truffle Cake, page 111

caramelized vanilla millefeuille

This is a very simple, quick dessert - using just a few pantry ingredients - and produces layers of caramelized flaky puff pastry leaves scattered with roasted nuts and sandwiched with a vanilla toffee cream. Dulce de leche is a wonderful caramel sauce available at Latino grocers and many supermarkets.

Preheat the oven to 400°F.

Spread the nuts on to a baking sheet and roast for 4–5 minutes (it won't take long as the oven is hot). Watch carefully so they don't burn. Cool, then chop. Line 2 or 3 baking sheets with parchment paper.

Roll out the pastry on a surface well dusted with confectioners' sugar to a thickness of about ¼". You need a large rectangle from which you will cut 3 equal-sized smaller rectangles. Pierce each pastry about 6 times with a fork. Refrigerate for about 30 minutes.

Alternatively, if you want a circular cake, cut out two 8" circles, using cake pans or plates as guides. Take the pastry trimmings, roll them out again and cut a third circle. Place all 3 on the baking sheets, pierce with a fork, and refrigerate for about 30 minutes.

When ready to bake, remove the pastry from the refrigerator, and sift the tops with confectioners' sugar. Bake until the sugar is melted and bubbling and the pastry is a lovely golden brown, 12-20 minutes. Watch carefully, as a few minutes too long and the pastry will burn. Let cool on the sheets for a minute or two, then peel off the parchment and cool on wire racks. These may be cooked a few hours in advance, though be sure only to add the filling an hour or so before serving.

Whip the cream to soft peaks and beat in 2 tablespoons dulce de leche and the vanilla. Place a pastry on a serving plate. Sandwich all 3 layers together, spreading the bottom and the middle layers with dulce de leche, then a layer of the whipped cream, and a sprinkling of nuts (if you wish, fill a pastry bag fitted with a large star tip with the cream, and pipe swirls over the first 2 layers). Finish by placing the top layer on the cake with a final dusting of confectioners' sugar and a final sprinkling of nuts. To serve, cut with a very sharp knife in a gentle sawing motion.

SERVES 8

1 cup (4 ounces) pistachios, pecans, or skinned hazelnuts
13 ounces store-bought butter puff pastry
2 tablespoons confectioners' sugar, plus more for garnish
1 cup heavy cream
1 cup dulce de leche
seeds from 1 vanilla bean, or 1 teaspoon vanilla extract
1 nylon pastry bag (optional)
1 large star pastry tip (optional)

strawberry, mint, and balsamic cheesecake

I find many cheesecakes too dense, but not this exceptionally light, summery version. The balsamic vinegar enhances the flavor of the strawberries wonderfully.

Preheat the oven to 350°F. Butter very well the bottom and sides of a 9" springform pan, making sure the flat side of the pan bottom is uppermost (the lipped side makes it hard to remove the cheesecake).

Mix the chocolate cookie crumbs, melted butter, and mint in a bowl until well combined. Lightly press into the pan with a spoon. Bake for 15 minutes, then let cool.

For the strawberry filling, simply mix everything together in a bowl and let stand for 1–2 hours for the strawberries to absorb the flavors. Drain the strawberries, reserving all the delicious juices.

For the cream cheese filling, pour 3 tablespoons cold water into a small, wide-bottomed heatproof bowl and sprinkle in the gelatin. Every single crystal must be wet, or it will turn lumpy later. Set the bowl in a saucepan of hot (not boiling) water and stir until every crystal has dissolved. Don't let it get too hot or it won't set properly.

In a small bowl, beat the cream cheese until smooth. In another bowl, lightly whip the cream and vanilla. Using an electric mixer and clean beaters, beat the egg yolks and sugar on high speed until thick, pale and doubled in volume. Carefully fold in the cream cheese, then the whipped cream. Mix the strawberry juices into the dissolved gelatin. Fold in a spoonful of the cream cheese mixture, then gently fold in the remaining mixture.

Spread the marinated strawberries over the center of the cookie base, ensuring they do not reach the edges. Spoon in the filling, smooth the top and refrigerate overnight to set.

To serve, dip a knife into hot water. Run the knife around the edge of the pan, then release the sides. Ease off the base with a dipped, hot metal spatula and transfer to a serving dish. Decorate with the sliced strawberries and mint sprigs.

SERVES 10–12

FOR THE BASE
1½ cups crushed chocolate graham crackers
4 tablespoons unsalted butter, melted, plus more for the pan
10 large mint leaves, finely chopped

FOR THE STRAWBERRY FILLING
2 cups thinly sliced strawberries
1 teaspoon balsamic vinegar
10 large mint leaves, finely chopped
1 tablespoons confectioners' sugar

FOR THE CREAM CHEESE FILLING
3 teaspoons unflavored powdered gelatin
9 ounces cream cheese, at room temperature
1 cup heavy cream
1 teaspoon vanilla extract
3 large egg yolks, at room temperature
¼ cup organic sugar

TO DECORATE
1 cup sliced strawberries
few sprigs of mint

sticky toffee cupcakes
with salted caramel buttercream

A beloved British dessert is brought up-to-date as a cupcake with salted caramel buttercream. There are two alternative toppings: the first involves making a caramel; the second, simply opening a jar of dulce de leche. The choice is yours, though the former will give a pleasing bitter edge. If you prefer an unsalted caramel buttercream, omit the salt and use unsalted butter.

Preheat the oven to 350°F. Place the liners into a muffin pan. In a heatproof bowl, pour 2/3 cup boiling water over the dates and let soak for 20 minutes. Then, with a fork, gently break up the dates and stir in the vanilla.

Sift the flour and baking soda into a bowl and set aside. Cream together the brown sugar and butter with an electric mixer on high speed for a good 5 minutes, until very light and fluffy. Add the eggs gradually, beating between each addition and adding in 1 tablespoon flour about halfway through to prevent curdling. Lastly, fold in the remaining flour and then the date mixture. Spoon into the cupcake paper liners and bake for 15–20 minutes (the tops should spring back when pressed with a finger). Let cool.

Meanwhile, make the buttercream. To make the caramel, stir the superfine sugar and 3 tablespoons water in a small, heavy-bottomed saucepan over low heat. Increase the heat to high and bring to a boil. Wait a few minutes, leaving the pan undisturbed but watching it like a hawk and, as soon as it changes to a wonderful caramel color (like strong tea) and is thicker, remove immediately from the heat. Stand well back, and gradually stir in the cream. Be very careful as it is searing hot and will splatter. It will react, or "seize," and you may think it has gone wrong; it hasn't. Keep stirring, adding the salt and the vanilla. Cool completely. (If using dulce de leche, simply mix it with the salt and vanilla.)

Cream the butter and confectioners' sugar for at least 5 minutes with an electric mixer. Add the cooled caramel (or dulce de leche). Put the buttercream in the pastry bag fitted with the star tip and pipe it on to the cakes, or spread it on with an icing spatula.

TO DECORATE see: Flying Insects, page 176

MAKES 12

FOR THE CAKES
12 cupcake paper liners
1 cup pitted and chopped dates
1 teaspoon vanilla extract
1¼ cups self-rising flour
1 teaspoon baking soda
¾ cup packed brown sugar
6 tablespoons unsalted butter, softened
2 large eggs, lightly beaten

FOR THE BUTTERCREAM
CARAMEL METHOD
2/3 cup superfine sugar
1/3 cup heavy cream, heated
½ teaspoon salt (or to taste)
1 teaspoon vanilla extract

DULCE DE LECHE METHOD
¼ cup dulce de leche
½ teaspoon salt (or to taste)
1 teaspoon vanilla extract

11 tablespoons salted butter, softened
1¾ cups confectioners' sugar, sifted
nylon pastry bag (optional)
medium or large star pastry tip (optional)

floral macaroons

These glamorous creations have become highly fashionable, and it's easy to see why. I've given four colors and flavors here – rose, lavender, orange, and pistachio – though as you improve, you could experiment with a wide range of colors and flavors. This is a tricky recipe, but do try it; if you follow the instructions carefully and read my perfect meringue tips (see page 71), it is very satisfying. The macaroons can be made ahead and freeze very well without their filling.

Line 2 baking sheets with parchment paper.

Sift the confectioners' sugar into a bowl and stir in the almond flour. With an electric mixer, beat the egg whites with a few drops of the chosen food color, starting slowly then increasing the speed, until soft peaks form. Slowly add the superfine sugar and vanilla and beat for about another minute until stiff. Gently fold in half of the almond mixture, then the other half, until smooth.

Spoon the mixture into the pastry bag and pipe 3/4" rounds on the trays, spacing them 1" or so apart. If there are any peaks, they are easily removed by very slightly moistening your finger with water and pressing down gently on to the peak. Set aside for about 30 minutes; they should have slightly skinned over. Meanwhile, preheat the oven to 325°F. Bake for 10–15 minutes with the door slightly ajar (I use a wooden spoon handle). The macaroons are ready when you can lift them off the parchment paper. Remove from the oven and cool on a wire rack. (If any stick to the parchment paper, rub a slightly damp cloth on the underside of the paper and they should detach.)

To make the rose, orange flower, or pistachio fillings, place the white chocolate in a bowl. Bring the cream to a boil in a small saucepan and pour it over the chocolate. Let stand for 1–2 minutes, then stir together until smooth, adding your chosen flavorings.

For the lavender filling, bring the lavender and cream to just below a boil, then set aside for 30 minutes to infuse. Strain, then return the cream to a boil, and proceed as above with the white chocolate.

Chill the fillings slightly. Whisk until thickened and use to sandwich the macaroons. They will keep in the refrigerator for a couple of days.

MAKES ABOUT 40 MACAROONS

1 cup confectioners' sugar
1 cup plus 3 tablespoons almond flour
3 large egg whites, at room temperature
a few drops of food coloring: pink, purple, orange, or green
4 teaspoons superfine sugar
1/2 teaspoon vanilla extract
nylon pastry bag fitted with a 1/2" wide plain tip

FOR THE FILLING
3 1/2 ounces Swiss white chocolate, finely chopped
1/3 cup heavy cream

ROSE
1 teaspoon rose water

ORANGE FLOWER
finely grated zest of 1 organic orange
1 teaspoon orange flower water

PISTACHIO
1 tablespoon ground unsalted pistachios

LAVENDER
1 tablespoon dried lavender

gilded chocolate tiffin

Fruit and nut chocolate bars will never taste the same again after you try these! A cross between a delicious chocolate and a good cookie, they can be served any time, but seem especially appropriate after dinner. The gold leaf adds luxury. I always make them at Christmas and they can be a very special gift, packed into a beautiful box. If you want to make bars, you will need silicone petit four molds.

Lightly butter an 8" square pan and line it with plastic wrap; this will make it easier to remove the tiffin later.

Preheat the oven to 350°F. Spread the nuts on to a baking sheet and roast in the oven for about 5 minutes, shaking once and watching carefully to make sure they don't burn. Let cool and chop into chunks.

Choose a bowl that will fit over a saucepan of simmering water, making sure the bottom of the bowl does not touch the water. Combine the butter, chocolate, and syrup in the bowl and melt over the water. Add the crushed cookies, nuts, and dried fruit to the mixture and stir until all is very well blended.

Spoon into the pan (or the silicone petits fours molds, if you are making bars) and refrigerate for at least 4 hours, until set. If you have used a pan, wait until the tiffin is set, then bring to room temperature to make it easier to cut (it might crack if too chilled). Cut into 36 squares, wiping the knife with paper towels between cuts.

The gold leaf needs to be applied very carefully in a room with no drafts. Place 1 tiffin square or bar at a time on to a work surface. Place the gold booklet close by and slide off 1 sheet, by gently holding the top 2 corners with the tips of the 2 paint brushes, using both hands. Static will cause the bristles to grip the sheet. Try not to breathe on or touch the gold before it is on the tiffin!

Loosely place the gold on a tiffin square, or wrap it around a bar, then smooth it down with a paint brush. If it tears, it doesn't matter, you can choose to patch it or leave it as it is with the chocolate showing through. You can either lay the gold randomly over the squares, leaving many of them plain, or wrap each bar completely in gold. Store in the refrigerator...or maybe the safe!

MAKES 36 SQUARES OR ABOUT
27 GOLDEN BARS

FOR THE TIFFIN
¾ cup (3 ounces) shelled, unsalted pistachios (or skinned hazelnuts or pine nuts)
7 tablespoons unsalted butter, diced, plus more for the pan
3½ ounces bittersweet chocolate (70% cacao), chopped
1 tablespoon golden syrup
1 cup finely crushed shortbread cookies (or even unsweetened cornflakes)
¾ cup finely chopped dried sour cherries (or dried blueberries, cranberries, apricots, or figs)

TO GILD
4–20 sheets of edible gold leaf, to taste and to budget!
2 small paint brushes

tiny meringues

These little meringues remind me of those my mother made. At any family celebration they were piled high, clouds of crispy white billows, oozing with cream, dusted with cocoa and finished with a crystallized violet. To me they were the most sublime dessert in the world.

Preheat the oven to 275°F and line 2 baking sheets with parchment paper.

Beat the egg whites and salt in a large bowl with an electric mixer. Start on low speed, then increase the speed until the whites form stiff peaks. Add the superfine sugar 1 tablespoon at a time, whisking between each addition, until stiff and glossy. Do not overmix. Sift in half the confectioners' sugar and very gently fold it in with a rubber spatula. Fold in the remaining sugar. Again, be careful not to overmix.

Fit a pastry bag with a medium star tip and fill with the meringue. Pipe 1½" diameter meringues on the baking sheets. (Or make little ovals by shaping the mixture between 2 teaspoons.) Bake for 25–35 minutes, until the undersides sound hollow when tapped. Carefully remove from the paper and cool on a wire rack.

Whip the cream lightly with the vanilla. Spread it over the bottoms of half the meringues, then sandwich with the others. Arrange on a serving plate, dust with cocoa and top each with a crystallized violet.

MAKES 50 MINI MERINGUES, OR
25 MERINGUE SANDWICHES

3 large egg whites, at room temperature
pinch of salt
scant ½ cup superfine sugar
¾ cup confectioners' sugar
large nylon pastry bag (optional)
medium star pastry tip (optional)
½ cup heavy cream
1 teaspoon vanilla extract
cocoa powder, to dust
25–30 crystallized violets

perfect meringues
Egg whites hate grease, so be punctilious about cleaning the bowl. Use metal, glass or ceramic, as plastic bowls are harder to degrease. Wipe the bowl with a cut lemon, then dry thoroughly before using. Egg whites don't like water, not even a drop.

Use uncracked organic eggs at room temperature; slightly older eggs give most volume. Beat with an electric mixer; it's hard work otherwise! Line baking sheets with parchment paper, not waxed paper or the meringues will stick. Dab a little meringue on the underside of the parchment to glue it to the baking sheet, if you wish.

gingerbread cookies

Once you have wrapped the dough in plastic wrap to chill, you can refrigerate it for a couple of days, or freeze for up to a month, so they are ready to bake at any time.

Sift the flour, ginger, cinnamon, and baking soda into a large bowl. Add the butter, cut into small chunks. Gently rub together with your fingertips until the mixture resembles fine breadcrumbs. Or, pulse all of these ingredients together in a food processor.

Add the sugar, syrup, molasses, yolk and zest and mix together until you have a firm dough. If it's too sticky, mix in a little more flour. Gather into a thick disk and wrap in plastic wrap. Chill for at least 1 hour.

Preheat the oven to 350°F. Line 2 baking sheets with parchment paper. Roll out the dough on a lightly floured surface to 1/4" thick, and cut out with a 2 1/2" round cutter. Bake for 10–15 minutes. The gingerbreads will have darkened a little.

Let cool on the sheets for a few minutes. Gently transfer to a wire rack to cool completely and crisp.

MAKES ABOUT 40

2⅔ cups all-purpose flour, plus more for rolling
4 teaspoons ground ginger
1 teaspoon ground cinnamon
½ teaspoon baking soda
⅔ cup salted butter, very slightly softened
¾ cup packed light brown sugar
3 tablespoons golden syrup
2 tablespoons molasses
1 large egg yolk
finely grated zest of 1 organic orange

TO DECORATE see: Autumn Leaves, page 196; Stained Glass Tree Cookies, page 199; Gingerbread Mobile, page 201

classic shortbread

My Scottish grandmother always baked shortbread with rice flour, but you can choose cornstarch if you prefer: rice flour will give a granulated, crunchy result, while cornstarch produces cookies that melt in the mouth. And be sure to use salted butter here. I always have a batch of these stored raw in the freezer so, at very short notice, I can fill the house with the scent of freshly baked shortbread. Use a selection of cutters; my favorites are hearts, stars, or simple rounds.

MAKES ABOUT 60

2¼ cups salted butter, softened
1 cup organic sugar, plus more to sprinkle
3½ cups all-purpose flour, plus more for rolling
1 cup cornstarch or white rice flour

Preheat the oven to 350°F. Using a handheld electric mixer on high speed, cream together the butter and sugar until light and fluffy. Gradually sift in the flour and cornstarch, stirring briefly between each addition, just until it binds together. Flour your hands and gently knead until just smooth (do not overwork). To make the dough easier to roll, wrap in plastic wrap and refrigerate for 30 minutes.

On a floured board, roll out the dough to about ¼" thick. Cut into your chosen shapes. I used a 1¾" heart-shaped cutter. (To freeze, lay the cut cookies between sheets of parchment paper in a freezer container. Defrost for 1 hour before baking.) Place the shortbreads on 2 baking sheets lined with parchment paper. Bake for 15–20 minutes. Sprinkle with sugar, then cool for 10 minutes on the sheets. Carefully transfer to a wire rack and cool completely.

flavorings
Add any of these to the butter and sugar before adding the flour:

vanilla seeds of 1 vanilla bean or ½ teaspoon vanilla extract

orange–cardamom finely grated zest of 1 organic orange, and ½ teaspoon freshly ground and sifted cardamom seeds

lemon–lavender finely grated zest of 1 organic lemon, finely grated, and 4 teaspoons fresh lavender flowers

cinnamon 2 teaspoons ground cinnamon

coffee 1 tablespoon instant coffee dissolved in 1 tablespoon boiling water, cooled

salt and pepper 24 turns of a pepper mill, or to taste; also sprinkle more pepper on top with the sugar

TO DECORATE see: Iced, Layered Shortbread, page 190

vanilla butter cookies

This is a very useful recipe as it is so versatile; it can be rolled quite thinly and holds its shape very well once baked. I used a 3" blossom cutter, but make any shape you prefer.

Sift the flour and salt into a bowl and set aside. Cream together the butter and sugar in a large bowl with an electric mixer until well combined and fluffy. Add the egg yolk and vanilla and mix in well, then work in the flour. Once the mixture comes together as a dough, dust your hands with flour and wrap it in plastic wrap. Chill for an hour (or up to a few days if more convenient) or freeze for up to a month. This dough can otherwise be tricky to work, especially in hot weather or a warm kitchen. When ready to bake, preheat the oven to 350°F.

Roll out the dough on a floured board to about ⅛" thick, using plenty of flour as it is quite sticky. (You could even roll it between 2 sheets of plastic wrap if that makes it easier for you.) Cut out into your preferred shapes and place on 2 baking sheets lined with parchment paper. Bake for 12–15 minutes until pale gold. Remove from the oven and let cool on the sheets for a few minutes. Carefully transfer the cookies to a wire rack. They will firm up as they cool. Cool completely.

Put the chocolate into a bowl over gently simmering water, ensuring the bottom of the bowl does not touch the water. Stir occasionally until melted. Cool slightly, then spoon into the pastry bag. Seal the bag and snip off the end. Drizzle the chocolate over the cookies to decorate.

MAKES 40

2¾ cups all-purpose flour, plus more for rolling

½ teaspoon salt

1 cup plus 2 tablespoons unsalted butter, softened

⅔ cup organic sugar

1 large egg yolk

1 teaspoon vanilla extract

3½ ounces bittersweet chocolate (50% cacao), chopped

1 disposable plastic pastry bag or freezer storage bag

TO DECORATE see: Doily Cookies, page 192; Easter Tree Cookies, page 195

decorate

cakes

23-carat gold cake

Real opulence on a plate: a dark, rich, luxurious chocolate cake encased in pure gold. Gold has been used to decorate food for centuries and has no taste or smell. This is a showstopper – an impressive centerpiece for an important occasion – and it may not cost quite as much as you think. If you choose to gild the top of the cake but not the sides, you will only have to buy a 25-sheet book of gold leaf; you'll need two books to encase the whole cake.

Place the cake on to its stand or serving plate.

The gold leaf needs to be applied very carefully in a room with no drafts. I find it easier to gild the sides of the cake first. Place the gold booklet close to the cake and slide off a sheet at a time, by gently holding the top 2 corners with the tips of the 2 paint brushes, using both your hands. Static will cause the bristles to grip on to the sheet. Try not to breathe on or touch the gold before it is on the cake!

With the tip of your finger, or using the back of a teaspoon, gently flatten the gold leaf on to the cake, then smooth it down with a brush.

If you would rather not use so much gilding, simply apply just 3 or 4 sheets, randomly laying them across the surface of the cake. The contrast of the dark chocolate and the gold looks stunning.

SERVES 16-20

Chocolate Celebration Cake with Ganache (page 14)

30 sheets loose 23-carat edible gold leaf (it comes in a book of 25 sheets, each about 3" square)
2 medium paint brushes

abstract expressionist

Transform your cake into a work of art! This cake is inspired by Jackson Pollock. We may not lay a huge sheet on the floor as he did, but we do have a small edible canvas covered in bright beet-colored icing. Using a pastry brush and a pastry bag, splatter and flick melted chocolate and icing all over the cake and release the artist in you. Ask the kids to help, if you dare…

Turn the cake upside down on to a serving plate, so the flat base becomes the top.

Place the confectioners' sugar in a bowl and gradually add the reserved beet juice from the cake recipe. If you would like a more shocking pink, you will need extra help from the food coloring: drop a little of it (remembering it is very strong) into the confectioners' sugar and stir until well blended and quite bright pink. Make sure you do not use too much, as the icing needs to remain thick enough to coat the back of a spoon. Pour it over the cake and allow to dry for at least 1 hour.

Place a small heatproof bowl over a saucepan of barely simmering water, making sure the bottom of the bowl does not touch the water. Add the white chocolate to the bowl and heat until it melts, stirring only very occasionally. Cool slightly, then spoon into a pastry bag. Repeat to melt the bittersweet chocolate. Snip the very ends of both bags. Dilute a little more pink food coloring in a dribble of water, making sure it remains darker than the icing covering the cake.

Now for the fun bit: drizzle and flick both colors of chocolate all over your cake canvas, then shake over the pink color using the pastry brush or toothbrush. Be as freeform as you like, until you have produced your very own edible masterpiece.

SERVES 10

Chocolate and Beet Cake (page 21), with reserved beet juice

2¼ cups confectioners' sugar, sifted
pink food coloring (optional)
1 ounce white chocolate, chopped
1 ounce bittersweet chocolate (60-70% cacao), chopped
2 disposable plastic pastry or storage bags
1 pastry brush or toothbrush

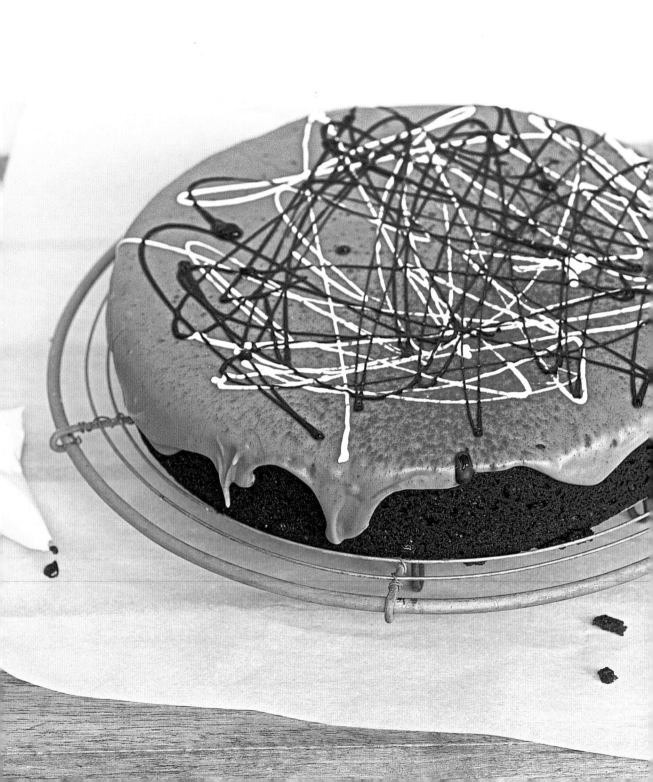

blackberry and geranium genoise

Scented geranium plants (Pelargonium, to be correct) are well worth hunting out. It's the oils in the leaves that make them special. Rub them between your fingers, or cook with them, and they release a wonderful aroma and flavor: lemon, orange, peppermint, even nutmeg and cinnamon! Attar of Roses is my favorite. In season, follow British food doyenne Elizabeth David's advice and combine geranium with blackberry; they have an extraordinary affinity.

To make the syrup, chop 3 of the geranium leaves. Place all the ingredients (reserving the last whole geranium leaf) in a small saucepan and simmer until reduced to about 2 tablespoons. Strain and let cool. Taste and add the whole geranium leaf if you like, or 1 teaspoon more rose water, as you prefer. Let stand for a day or so.

Space out the 12 geranium leaves evenly in the base of the paper-lined cake tin, then pour in the batter and bake as described (see page 34). Let cool, remove the paper and the leaves.

Slice in half horizontally and sprinkle the cut surfaces with the syrup. Fill with the cream filling and the blackberries. Sandwich together and sift confectioners' sugar over the top. Decorate with more blackberries, sprigs of sweet geranium leaves and flowers.

SERVES 8

Genoise batter and cream filling, kept separate (page 34)

FOR THE SYRUP
4 scented geranium leaves
1 tablespoon rose water, or to taste
1/4 cup granulated sugar
juice of half a lemon

12 small scented geranium leaves (from one variety), plus more with flowers to decorate
1 1/2 cups blackberries, plus more to decorate
confectioners' sugar, for garnish

eastern fantasy

This enchanting cake has a branch of fabric hydrangea and berries with a little bird sitting in the foliage. Layered organza, velvet and bejewelled ribbons hug the sides.

Color the fondant the day before, making a pale pistachio green with the 3 food coloring pastes (see page 11).

To cover the cake with fondant, remove any star anise flowers from the top and turn it upside down on a clean work surface, so the flat bottom is uppermost. Warm the jam gently in a small saucepan. Push it through a sieve and brush it all over the cake.

Dust a clean work surface and a rolling pin with confectioners' sugar and roll out the fondant into a circle slightly larger than the diameter of the cake and sides and no thinner than $1/4$". Keep moving the fondant and run an icing spatula underneath it or dust with more confectioners' sugar as necessary, as it is so frustrating if it sticks to the work surface.

Lift the fondant on to the cake with your hands (or wrap it loosely around the rolling pin) and place it on the cake. Rub all over and smooth around the sides until you have a good shape, then cut away the excess fondant. Run an icing spatula under the cake and lift it on to the final plate, board or cake stand. Let the fondant set for an hour or 2, if possible. It can be decorated immediately, but be careful not to dent the icing.

Using the royal icing, attach the branch to the top of the cake, and secure the 3 ribbons with a dab of royal icing at the back. Push the bird in among the flowers.

SERVES 8–10

Star Anise, Almond and
  Clementine Cake (page 40)
  with syrup

2¼ pounds white fondant
olive green, ivory, and mint green
  food coloring pastes, as needed
¼ cup apricot jam
confectioners' sugar, for rolling
¼ cup royal icing in a parchment
  paper cone (see page 9)
branch of artificial intertwined
  berries and hydrangea
about 1 yard 2¼" wide pale lilac
  organza ribbon
about 1 yard ¾" wide silver
  bejewelled ribbon
about 1 yard ½" wide burgundy
  velvet ribbon
1 artificial bird, secured on a
  wooden toothpick

mosaic cake

Very striking designs can be made with simple, graphic patterns of candies and chocolates. Here, the color palette has been limited to give more impact. Children, especially, will love to create their own designs.

Turn the cake upside down and split in half horizontally. Spread most of the lime buttercream over the cut surface and place the other cake on top so the flat bottom becomes the top. Spread a very thin layer of the remaining buttercream around the sides (this will help the fondant stick to the cake).

Roll out the fondant on a clean board, lightly dusting both the board and a rolling pin with a little confectioners' sugar to stop it from sticking. Roll into a rough square about 1/4" thick and slightly larger than the width of the cake and sides. Lift it with your hands or loosely roll it around the rolling pin, place it over the cake and gently smooth around the sides, rubbing it with your hands. Try not to stretch the fondant and work as quickly as you can as it will dry out fairly rapidly. Cut away any excess and, provided it is still clean, seal in a plastic bag and store at room temperature; you can reuse it another time. Leave to dry for a few hours or, even better, overnight.

Using the royal icing, stick on the chocolate candies; it is a good idea to work out the pattern first on a board.

Finish by wrapping the ribbon around the cake and sticking down the seam at the back with a dab of royal icing.

SERVES 10

Sticky Ginger Cake with
    Lime Buttercream (page 28),
    kept separate

2¼ pounds white fondant
confectioners' sugar, for rolling
¼ cup royal icing in a parchment
    paper cone (see page 9)
sugar-coated chocolate candies,
    as needed
1 yard ¾" wide spotted ribbon

gala cake

Flags and bunting decorate this four-tiered candy-striped cake. I have used fresh raspberry and blueberry fruit purees, lemon curd, and lime to flavor the buttercream, but you could try strawberry, mango, passion fruit, or black currant purees, or even use good-quality jams to create each flavor instead. The bunting and flags can be made well ahead of time. I find it easiest to choose their colors first, then coordinate the buttercream colors to match.

For the flags, glue the scraps of ribbon and paper on to the toothpicks. To make the bunting, cut out paper triangles and glue them on to the ribbon.

Make the 4 colored buttercreams. Divide the buttercream equally between 4 bowls. Make the raspberry puree by gently warming the berries in a small saucepan, crushing with a fork, then sieving to remove the seeds. Let cool. Make the blueberry puree in the same way, adding 1 tablespoon water to the pan. Add the raspberry puree to 1 bowl of buttercream, the blueberry puree to another and the lemon curd to the third. Finally add the lime zest and juice and a little green food coloring to the last bowl.

Take the 4 Victoria sponge cakes (or split them horizontally if you have chosen to bake 2 large cakes instead). Spread a different buttercream between each of the 4 layers, topping with the blueberry.

Place the cake on its stand. Arrange the flags and windmills over the top and attach the bunting to the stand with the sticky tape.

SERVES 16

2 recipes Victoria Sponge Cake
    (page 24)

glue
scraps of contrasting ribbon and
    paper
8 wooden toothpicks
about 5 feet ¼" wide ribbon
    (or enough to wrap twice round
    your cake stand)
Vanilla Buttercream (page 9)
1 cup raspberries
1 cup blueberries
⅓ cup store-bought lemon curd
finely grated zest of 1 lime, and
    juice of ½ lime
green food coloring paste
2 paper windmills (optional)
double-sided sticky tape

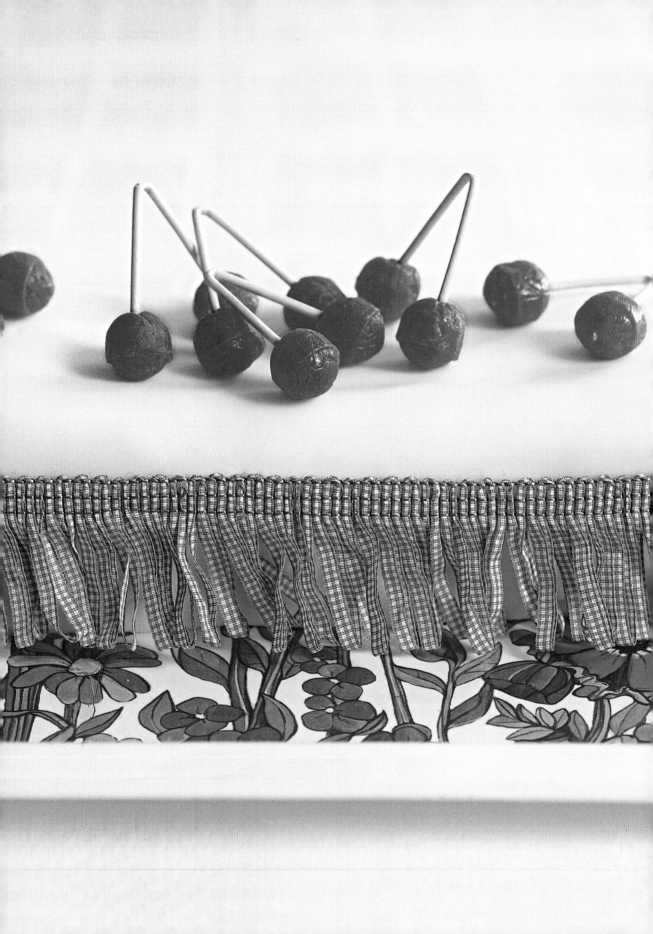

summer cherries

It is said that you can trace old Roman roads in Britain by the wild cherry trees that grew up from stones spat out by legions as they marched! Here is a very simple cake decorated with cherry lollipops as a tribute to the legions.

Place the cake flat base up on a clean board or work surface. Brush the jam all over it. Lightly sprinkle a clean, flat surface with confectioners' sugar (sprinkle your rolling pin too) and roll out the fondant into a rectangle no thinner than 1/4" and slightly larger than the cake and sides.

Lift the fondant with your hands or loosely roll it around the rolling pin, place it over the cake and gently smooth around the sides, covering the cake. Do not stretch the fondant and work as quickly as you can, as it will dry out fairly rapidly. Cut away any excess and, provided it is clean, seal it in a plastic bag at room temperature for future use. Smooth the cake and sides all over with the palms of your hands; any lumps or bumps can hopefully be eliminated now.

Arrange the lollipops on the cake surface, sticking them on with a little royal icing. Attach the fringe, again using the royal icing to adhere, at the back of the cake.

SERVES 8

Cherry and Marzipan Cake (page 50), baked in a loaf pan

3 tablespoons apricot jam, warmed and sieved
confectioners' sugar, for rolling
2¼ pounds white fondant
6 Twin Cherry Lollipops (see page 207)
¼ cup royal icing in a parchment paper cone (see page 9)
1 yard 1¾" wide green or red gingham fringe

sweet shop

A feast for a child's eye (just don't expect the cake to be eaten first). Any selection of candies can be used; pile them high! I have used the old-fashioned kinds that I used to buy on Saturdays as a child. My own children love them too.

Place the cake on a clean board. Lightly sprinkle a work top with confectioners' sugar (sprinkle your rolling pin, too) and roll out the fondant into a circle no thinner than $1/4$" and slightly larger than the diameter of the cake and sides.

Lift the fondant with your hands or loosely wrap it around the rolling pin, place it over the cake and gently smooth around the sides, covering the cake. Do not stretch the fondant and work as quickly as you can, as it will dry out fairly rapidly. Cut away any excess fondant and seal it in a plastic food bag at room temperature for future use (providing it doesn't have fudge icing on it). Smooth the top and sides all over with the palms of your hands; any lumps, bumps or blemishes can hopefully be eliminated now.

Arrange the candies randomly over the surface of the cake, with the jelly beans around the base, sticking them all on with the royal icing.

SERVES 8

Family Chocolate Cake with
    Fudge Icing (page 17), iced
    over the top and sides

confectioners' sugar, for rolling
$2 1/4$ pounds white fondant
a selection of candies (I used 2
    candy canes; 1 sugar mouse, 2
    candy bracelets and 1 necklace;
    1 small packet of sugar hearts;
    6 striped marshmallows; 3–4
    large sweet/tart candies; 40–50
    jelly beans)
$1/4$ cup royal icing in a parchment
    paper cone (see page 9)

a summer garden

This is one of the simplest decorations in this book and shows a beautiful cake does not need to be complicated or time-consuming. Any seasonal, edible flowers could be used; try primroses, violets, chrysanthemums, or daisies.

Preheat the oven to 325°F. Spread the pistachios on to a baking sheet and roast for 5–10 minutes, shaking once and watching carefully to make sure they don't burn. Let cool, then coarsely chop.

Make a white chocolate ganache with the chocolate, cream and rose water, using the method on page 18 (this makes twice that amount).

Turn the cake upside down so the flat base becomes the top and split it in half. Fill with a layer of the ganache, then with the raspberries, and top with the second layer of cake. Spread the top and sides with the remaining ganache.

Press the roasted pistachios all around the side of the cake and, when ready to serve, decorate the top with the edible flowers tightly packed together. Stunning.

SERVES 8

White Chocolate and Cardamom Rose Water Cake (page 18), baked in a round pan

1 cup (4 ounces) shelled unsalted pistachios
7 ounces Swiss white chocolate, finely chopped
$2/3$ cup heavy cream
1 tablespoon rose water
$1\frac{1}{2}$ cups fresh raspberries
40–50 whole edible and unsprayed flowers (I used cornflowers, pinks, nasturtiums, marigolds, borage, and very small sunflowers)

giant cupcake

Instead of making a batch of cupcakes, why not confuse everyone and make a monster! It is a little wasteful because of the need to shape the coffee cakes, but enjoy sampling as you sculpt them. Cook's treat!

Preheat the oven to 350°F. Lightly butter two 6 x 3" cake pans and line the bottoms with parchment paper. Pour the batter into the pans and smooth. Bake for 30–35 minutes. Let cool completely. Freeze for about an hour (this makes it much easier to shape).

Take 1 cake and, with a very sharp knife, cut down the sides at an angle so that it is narrower at the base (to mimic a cupcake liner). Slice the cake horizontally and fill with buttercream, spreading it on the top surface, too. Take the second cake and place on top. Cut it into a dome, then slice it in half horizontally and fill with buttercream.

Spread a layer of buttercream around the sides of the bottom cake and put the remainder into the pastry bag fitted with the star tip. Ice the top with swirls of buttercream, just as you would a small cupcake.

Arrange the chocolate cookies vertically all around the sides of the cake for the "cupcake case," pressing them into the buttercream. Sprinkle the chocolate coffee beans over the cake and place the candle on top.

SERVES 10-12

Coffee and Hazelnut Cake batter (page 37)

Vanilla Buttercream (see page 9)
nylon pastry bag
large star pastry tip
9 ounces milk or dark chocolate rolled wafer cookies (such as Pirouette)
20 chocolate-covered coffee beans
tall (4") birthday candle

rose petal heart

An exquisite combination of white chocolate, cardamom, rose water and raspberries, this cake is temptingly strewn with crystallized petals and white chocolate curls. Both can be made a few days ahead, then stored in dry conditions in a cardboard box at room temperature.

Split the cake horizontally, spoon in the filling and the fresh raspberries, then turn it upside down on to a cake stand. Place the confectioners' sugar into a bowl and gradually add the rose water, mixing all the time until the icing is thick enough to coat the back of a spoon. Pour over the cake and let it drizzle down the sides. Let set for an hour or so.

To make the chocolate curls, place a small heatproof bowl over a saucepan of gently simmering water, making sure the bottom of the bowl does not touch the water. Add the white chocolate to the bowl and heat until it melts, stirring only very occasionally. Pour it on to a plastic board or a piece of marble, and spread out with an icing spatula. Let set; a short spell in the refrigerator will help.

Run a sharp fine knife at a 45-degree angle across the chocolate (or use a vegetable peeler) and it will curl. Too cold and it won't work; too soft and it will need 15 minutes or so back in the refrigerator. You'll have to experiment.

Scatter the cake with the chocolate curls, then with the rose petals.

SERVES 8

White Chocolate and Cardamom Rose Water Cake, baked in a heart-shaped pan, with filling, kept separate (page 18)

1½ cups fresh raspberries
¾ cup confectioners' sugar, sifted
about 3 tablespoons rose water
3½ ounces white chocolate, finely chopped
12 crystallized pink rose petals (see page 107)

pansy wreath

This enchanting cake is so summery with its circlet of violas and pansies. In spring it would look equally pretty decorated with crystallized primulas.

Place the cake upside down on to your serving plate or cake stand.

Sift the confectioners' sugar into a small bowl and stir in 1½–2 tablespoons water and a tiny amount of purple food coloring. The icing should be thick enough to coat the back of a spoon. Spoon it over the cake and allow it to drizzle down the sides.

Arrange the violas and pansies in a circle, using the royal icing to affix them, if you like, then place a few in the middle of the cake. It's as simple as that.

SERVES 6

Very Lemony Crunch Cake with syrup (page 31)

1¼ cups confectioners' sugar
purple food coloring
20–25 crystallized small violas and pansies (page 107)
3 tablespoons royal icing in a parchment paper cone (see page 9) (optional)

how to make crystallized flowers and leaves

A quick and stunning decoration that requires very little equipment, just a quiet hour and a bit of patience. These should keep for up to a week in a dry place. Use unsprayed flowers that are completely dry. You can use reconstituted dried egg whites or meringue powder instead of fresh egg whites, if you wish.

Line a baking sheet with parchment paper.

Place the egg white in a bowl and the sugar in another. Hold the flower, petal or leaf at the base and paint with egg white, ensuring you cover every fold. Gently sprinkle on the sugar, again making sure every surface is covered, then shake off the excess.

If crystallizing whole roses, push a fine florists' wire through the base of the bloom, then hook the wire over a tall glass. Let stand overnight in a dry, warm place. The flower will dry while hanging.

Lay sugared petals or leaves on the lined sheet and let stand overnight in a dry, warm place (an empty cupboard is ideal), until brittle.

Store in an airtight container, lined and interleaved with parchment paper. They are very fragile, so only make a couple of layers.

MAKES AS MANY AS YOU WANT

egg white, whisked until foamy
superfine sugar
edible and unsprayed flowers
    and leaves, such as whole
    roses or rose petals, violas,
    pansies, violets, mimosa,
    cowslips, pinks, primroses,
    lavender, sweet geranium
    leaves, mint leaves
small paint brush
florists' wire (optional)

rose garden

This is the cake to celebrate summer, when the days are long, the sun is high in the sky and the scent of fresh-mown grass is in the air. Summoning up memories of lazy afternoons in the garden, and adorned with full-blown crystallized roses, it's a magical cake.

Invert the cake on to a cake stand or plate, so that the flat bottom forms the top surface.

Sift the confectioners' sugar into a bowl and gradually add the orange juice, mixing all the time until it is thick enough to coat the back of the spoon. Pour over the cake, letting it drizzle down the sides.

Allow to set for at least 1 hour, then carefully arrange the crystallized roses in the center.

SERVES 8

Pistachio and Orange Blossom
    Cake (page 38), with its syrup

1¾ cups confectioners' sugar
about 3 tablespoons fresh orange
    juice
3 crystallized roses (see page
    107)

easter chocolate truffle cake

If you haven't already eaten too many chocolate eggs, this would be a perfect ending to Easter lunch, or served at tea time. The sugar eggs can be made weeks ahead, and the cake a day or two in advance then assembled shortly before serving. Consult the suppliers list (page 207) for sources for egg molds.

To make the sugar eggs, place the sugar in a bowl. Mix in 1–2 teaaspoons water and mix; it will feel a bit like wet sand. Pack it into the egg mold. Level off with an icing spatula. Let set for about 24 hours, until the eggs harden.

Divide the royal icing between 2 small bowls. Leave 1 bowl of icing white and color the remaining icing yellow. Transfer each icing to disposable plastic bag and snip off each tip.

Turn the mold upside down and lightly tap on a work surface. The egg halves should drop out. Stick the halves together with a little white royal icing. Decorate by sticking on the sugar flowers, ribbon roses, or bows with royal icing, then pipe on little yellow polka dots.

When you are ready to serve, place the cake on to a serving plate or cake stand. Arrange the decorated eggs in a circle with the foliage.

SERVES 12

Dark Chocolate Mousse Cake
  (page 58)

½ cup superfine sugar
1 plastic egg mold (for 9 sugar
  eggs, each about 1¼" long)
3 tablespoons royal icing in a
  parchment paper cone (see
  page 9)
yellow food coloring paste
selection of tiny sugar flowers,
  ribbon roses and little bows
fresh (preferably edible and
  unsprayed) foliage, such as
  chrysanthemum leaves

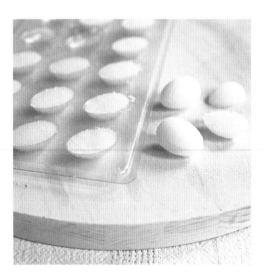

maypole

For centuries, the maypole has been an expression of joy
and hope celebrating the start of spring. You could even
cover the whole cake with a carpet of sugar flowers. I have
specified the ribbons I used, but do take these instructions
only as a guide.

To make the maypole, twist the white ribbon all around the tube
tightly and glue at both ends. Next, take the 6 lengths of colored ⅛"
ribbon and, starting at one end, wind them together tightly round and
round the tube. Again, the ribbons need to be fastened at the bottom
of the pole (I took them inside the tube and glued firmly). At the top
end, secure them inside the pole, then cascade them out.

Make a tassel for the top by taking 2 x 6" lengths of each of the 6
colored ⅛" ribbons, tying together very firmly and wedging into the
top of the pole. Tie 6 tiny bows in different colors, using about 6" each
of the ⅛" ribbons.

Now, turn the cake upside down, split it horizontally and sandwich
with some of the buttercream. Place the other half on top so the flat
bottom is uppermost, then spread buttercream over the top and sides.

Lightly sprinkle a clean, flat surface with confectioners' sugar
(sprinkle your rolling pin too) and roll out the fondant into a circle no
thinner than ¼" and slightly larger than the diameter of the cake and
sides. Lift the fondant with your hands or loosely roll it around the
rolling pin, place it over the cake and gently smooth around the sides,
covering the cake. Cut away any excess and smooth the cake all over
with your hands; any lumps or bumps can be eliminated now.

Find the center of the cake and push in the maypole, using a little royal
icing to secure. Take the 6 cascading ribbons from the top of the pole
and, using royal icing, secure at 6 equidistant points at both the edge
and base of the cake. Trim the excess fondant. Stick a little contrasting
bow at the 6 points around the cake and attach the flowered ribbon
around the base. Adhere the sugar flowers round the bottom of the
maypole, again using the royal icing as 'glue.'

SERVES 8

Orange Drizzle Cake (page 32)
½ recipe Orange Buttercream
   (see page 9)

1 yard ½" wide white satin ribbon
1 plastic or cardboard tube,
   about 6" long and ½" in
   diameter
glue
6 x 4 foot lengths ⅛" wide ribbon
   in different colors
confectioners' sugar, for rolling
2¼ pounds white fondant
3 tablespoons royal icing in a
   parchment paper cone (see
   page 9)
2½ feet 4" wide ribbon (mine was
   green with white flowers)
5 small sugar flowers

summer berry
rose-scented meringue

All the aromas, flavors and colors of summer are celebrated in this cake. Tiers of crisp, candy-striped meringue with a marshmallowy center, oozing with a subtle rose-vanilla cream, packed with berries and strewn with rose petals.

Spread out the 3 circles of meringue on parchment paper-lined baking sheets as described on page 55. Dip the end of a wooden toothpick, or a teaspoon handle, into the pink food coloring (if using food coloring paste, dilute with a very little water first) and swirl over the meringue. Bake as described on page 55. The circles should be crispy and dry on the outside and may be a bit cracked, which is fine. Leave the oven door slightly ajar and let cool completely.

Whip the cream until soft peaks form, adding the sugar, vanilla, and rose water. Place the largest meringue circle on a cake stand or serving plate. Spread with some cream, sprinkle over some berries, add a little more cream, then place the medium meringue on top. Repeat with the remaining cream and berries and top with the smallest disk. Sift confectioners' sugar on top, and a little glitter, if desired, and toss on the rose petals, letting them fall casually on and around.

SERVES 12

FOR THE MERINGUE
Exotic Fruit Chewy Meringue
    (page 55), unbaked

pink food coloring paste or liquid
    food coloring

FOR THE FILLING
2 cups heavy cream
1/3 cup confectioners' sugar, plus
    more for sifting
2 teaspoons vanilla extract, or
    seeds from 1 vanilla bean
2 teaspoons rose water
about 4 cups berries of
    your choice: raspberries,
    blueberries, red currants,
    black currants, blackberries,
    sliced strawberries, and pitted
    cherries
clear edible glitter (optional)
15–20 unsprayed rose petals

pink iced heart

What more does a girl need for a special celebration? This is simplicity itself to make. Remember that, as gorgeous as they may be, in the U.S. the FDA has stated that dragees are just for decoration.

Preheat the oven to 350°F.

Butter well a large heart-shaped pan, 9" at its widest part, and line the bottom with parchment paper. Pour in and spread the batter. Bake for 30–35 minutes. When a wooden toothpick inserted into the center comes out clean, it is ready. Let cool slightly in the pan. Turn out on to a wire rack, remove the paper and cool completely.

Make the buttercream by beating the butter, confectioners' sugar and vanilla for 5 minutes with an electric mixer on high speed, until really soft and fluffy. Add drops of the pink food coloring. Any shade is fine: you can pick a baby pink, a medium or, as we did for this photograph, a strong, full-on girlie tone.

Turn the cake upside down, split it horizontally and, using an icing spatula, spread some of the pink buttercream over the cut surface, then add a layer of jam. Place the other half of the cake on top and spread the rest of the buttercream all over the top and sides, making it as smooth as possible.

Immediately, press a collar of the dragees all around the outside edge (the icing will start to set if you wait too long) and sprinkle them all with a little glitter. Finish by placing the candles on the cake, if you like.

SERVES 8

Victoria Sponge Cake batter
  (page 24)

1 cup unsalted butter, plus more
  for the pan
2¾ cups confectioners' sugar,
  sifted
1 teaspoon vanilla extract
pink food coloring
¼ cup raspberry or strawberry
  jam
about ⅔ cup multicolored dragees
  (I added a few larger and tiny
  silver dragees, but it's fine to
  use all one size)
clear edible glitter
3 pink or purple birthday candles
  and candle holders (optional)

party cake with streamers

Perfect for all ages. The little 'cake' on top are made out of sugar. You can make them a few weeks ahead if you like; store in a cardboard box at room temperature.

Place the chocolate cake on the board. To make the little cakes, simply place a disc of fondant into each case. Make up a small amount of icing by very gradually adding 2 tablespoons water to the confectioners' sugar until it is thick enough to coat the back of a spoon, then divide between 3 bowls. Color the first pink, another green, and the third yellow. Spoon into the paper cases, making 4 of each color, then top with the colored sprinkles. Let stand at least 4 hours, or until they are set. Arrange the sugar cakes on the large cake.

Curl the ribbons by running the blade of a blunt knife along the length of each, then lay these streamers casually over the cake, allowing them to cascade down the sides.

SERVES 8

Family Chocolate Cake with
  Fudge Icing (page 17), iced
  over the top and sides

one 10" round aluminum foil cake
  board
4 ounces white fondant
12 aluminum foil candy liners
1¾ cups confectioners' sugar,
  sifted
pink food coloring paste
green food coloring paste
yellow food coloring paste
3 teaspoons colored sprinkles
  (¼ teaspoon per cake)
7–8 yards metallic ribbon, cut
  into 1 yard strips

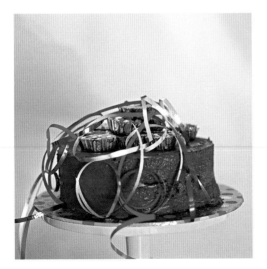

ribbon roses

These roses are very quick and easy and there's no sewing.
I used realistic colors but yours can be in crazy shades, if you
prefer. They can, of course, be made months ahead.

Color the fondant the day before, if possible (see page 11). I made a
pale buttery tone, using the 2 shades listed here.

Warm the jam gently in a saucepan, sieve it and brush all over the
cake. Sprinkle a clean work surface with confectioners' sugar and roll
out the fondant into a circle roughly as big as the diameter and sides of
the cake, and no thinner than ¼". Keep moving the fondant and run
an icing spatula underneath it, adding more confectioners' sugar if
necessary. Lift the fondant on to the cake with your hands, smooth it
all over and cut away any excess. Run the spatula under the cake and
lift it on to your cake stand or plate. Let set for at least an hour or so.

To make a ribbon rose, take 1 yard of wired ribbon and, as close as
possible to one end, tie a small tight knot. From the other end, pull
the wire out; the ribbon will ruffle. Ease it along towards the knotted
end. Keep pulling on the wire gently until all the ribbon is ruffled.
Starting at the knot end, twist the ruffled ribbon round and round the
knot to form the central bud and 'petals.' Secure with
the wire tightly around the base and cut off any excess.
Repeat with the other 2 ribbons.

Wrap the organza ribbon around the cake and attach
with a dab of royal icing at the back. Stick the ribbon
roses in the center and tuck in the artificial leaves.

SERVES 8

Cherry and Marzipan Cake (page
  50), baked in a round pan

2¼ pounds white fondant
peach and/or yellow food coloring
  paste
¼ cup apricot jam
confectioners' sugar, for rolling
three 1 yard lengths 1½" wide
  wired ribbon, in different colors
about 32 inches 1¼" wide green
  organza ribbon
3 tablespoons royal icing (page 9)
3 artificial leaves

fresh petal confetti cake

No special equipment, time or expertise required, but serve it soon after decorating, or the petals start to wilt. The only secret is in your choice of edible unsprayed petals. I used cornflowers, lavender, rose petals and marigolds. I filled and covered the cake with Lavender and Lemon Buttercream (see page 146), but plain lemon or vanilla Buttercream (see page 9) is just as good.

If you have chosen to bake in 2 tins, place the bottom half of the cake on a work surface and spread with the lemon curd and a layer of buttercream. If you have made just 1 deeper cake, split it horizontally with a serrated knife, invert the top half on a work surface and spread with the lemon curd and a layer of buttercream. Top with the remaining cake, inverted so the flat bottom is uppermost, and cover the top and sides with buttercream. Try to make it as smooth as possible.

Roll up the petals (not the lavender as they are tiny flowers) and slice very finely into strips with a sharp knife, or snip with a pair of scissors. Keep the petals fresh for an hour or so, if needed, by laying them out on a damp cloth or paper towels.

When ready to decorate, take a small handful of petals at a time and press into the buttercream all around the sides of the cake. To finish, scatter the remaining petal confetti on top.

SERVES 8-10

Victoria Sponge Cake (page 24)

$\frac{1}{3}$ cup store-bought lemon curd
$\frac{1}{2}$ recipe Lemon and Lavender
  Buttercream (see page 146)
selection of unsprayed edible
  petals in contrasting colors:
  try lavender, cornflowers,
  rose petals, marigolds,
  chrysanthemums, pansies,
  sunflowers, primulas, daisies,
  carnations, or pinks

fluttering butterflies

Exquisite fabric and feather butterflies on wires are widely available at floral suppliers and craft shops in an assortment of colors and designs. They will "fly" over your cake to give instant impact.

Color the fondant the day before, if possible, using the 2 listed food colorings, until you have achieved your desired shade (see page 11).

Gently warm the jam, sieve it, then brush all over the cake. Sprinkle a clean work surface with confectioners' sugar and roll out the fondant into a circle roughly the diameter of the cake and sides and no thinner than 1/4". Keep moving the fondant and run an icing spatula underneath it, adding a little confectioners' sugar if necessary. Lift the fondant on to the cake with your hands (or wrap loosely around the rolling pin) and place it on the cake. Rub all over and smooth around the side until you have a good shape, then cut away any excess fondant.

Run a knife under the cake and lift on to your final cake stand or plate. If you wish, press a blossom pattern into the fondant about 30 times. Let set for at least an hour or two if you can.

Wrap the ribbons loosely around the cake, twining them together, and tie at the back or cut neatly and glue with a little royal icing. Twist all the butterfly wires together and attach to the ribbons at the back of the cake. Bend the wires over the cake so the butterflies appear to be fluttering above it.

SERVES 8

Cherry and Marzipan Cake (page 50), baked in a round pan

2¼ pounds white fondant
tangerine or apricot food coloring paste
burgundy food coloring paste
4 tablespoons apricot jam
confectioners' sugar, for rolling
½" plunger blossom cutter (optional)
two 1 yard 1½" wide ribbons in contrasting colors to coordinate with the butterflies
1 yard ⅝" wide braided ribbon
3 tablespoons royal icing in a parchment paper cone (see page 9) (optional)
6–8 butterflies on wires (mine were about 3¼" wide)

bollywood extravaganza

This exotic cake is inspired by my yearly visits to India. Its dazzling array of fondant full-blown roses in clashing colors reminds me of sizzling–hot spices. Even if your roses are not perfect, their sheer impact in these vibrant hues, sprinkled with glitter and encircled with bejewelled ribbon, will create a stunning centerpiece.

The roses can be made a few weeks ahead. Divide the fondant into 5 portions (this quantity makes about 40 2" roses).

When coloring the fondant, the use of black is optional. It does make a more interesting color, but use literally a pinprick when required. Mix 5 different colors of fondant (see page 11). Create a deep red with poppy red, egg yellow and black; a bright pink with burgundy, pink and black; a light pink with burgundy; a bright orange with poppy red and egg yellow; a lighter orange with canary yellow and black. Let the fondant rest overnight (it will be much easier to mold).

Make 8 roses in each color (see page 129). Sprinkle with glitter and store in a covered box at room temperature.

When ready to assemble, place the cake on the serving plate. Arrange the roses all over the top.

Finish by wrapping the ribbon around the cake, using a blob of extra ganache at the back to hold it in place.

SERVES 16-20

Chocolate Celebration Cake with Ganache (page 14) made with chile-flavoured chocolate

2½ pounds white fondant
a variety of food coloring pastes, such as poppy red, egg yellow, black, burgundy, pink, and canary yellow
clear edible glitter
1¼ yards of 1½" wide ribbon, preferably bejewelled or ornate

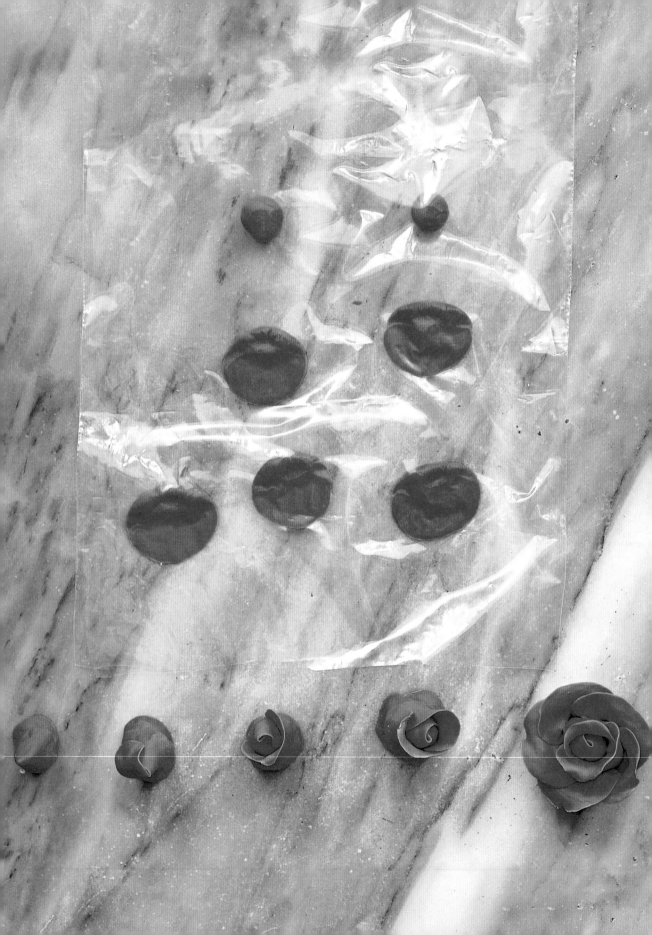

how to make fondant roses

It is well worth mastering how to make these; don't worry,
I have never met anyone who can't! It requires no special
equipment, just a bit of patience and perseverance. In nature
no two roses are the same, and chances are yours won't
be either. As you become more experienced you'll find it
easier, and your roses will very quickly improve.

The darker the fondant – and hence the more food coloring paste
you have used – the softer it will be, and harder to mold. So, for your
first attempts, use pale colors. (Liquid food coloring may make it too
soft.) Once you have kneaded and colored the sugarpaste (see page
11) you may need to adjust the texture: if it is too soft, add a little
confectioners' sugar; if too dry, add a tiny amount of shortening.
If possible, color the fondant the day before you need it, as it will
be much easier to work. Store fondant in a sealed plastic bag, and
finished roses in a cardboard box (not an airtight container or they
will sweat), both at room temperature. Never store them in the
refrigerator. Fondant roses will keep for months.

Take 1¹/₂ ounces of the fondant. Split a plastic bag open and place on
a flat work top. Tear off one-third of the fondant and roll it into a
ball in your hands, then into a cone. Flatten the base on to the work
surface, then indent it to shape a cone on top of a rough ball.

Mold 7 or 8 balls (to become the petals) from the remaining fondant
and lay them on one side of the bag. Fold over the other side on top
and flatten each ball until quite thin. The thinner it is, the finer the
petal, but don't be too ambitious at first.

Very gently peel back the plastic. Take a petal at a time and, with the
side you pressed on uppermost, mold it around the cone, completely
covering the top. Take the second petal and place it centrally over the
seam of the first (again, with the side you pressed on uppermost),
molding it around the cone. Place the third petal directly opposite.
Tweak out all the petals as you work, to look like a real rose. You have
now made a rosebud!

Fold the remaining 4 or 5 petals around the rosebud in the same way,
each overlapping the last. Again, tweak out these petals as you work.
With a small knife, cut away the base at a slight angle. You can use
these trimmings when you make the next rose.

MAKES AS MANY AS YOU WANT

about 1¹/₂ ounces fondant for
   each rose
confectioners' sugar, as needed
vegetable shortening, as needed

christmas trees

A little forest of fondant trees with candy cane trunks and sparkling sugar snow adorn this festive cake.

Two days before serving, color 10½ ounces of the fondant 2 shades of green, making the darker tone first (see page 11). Seal in separate plastic bags. Turn the cake upside down on to a serving plate or cake drum, securing with a dab of jam. If there are any holes or the cake is a slightly dodgy shape, correct it now with bits of marzipan. Once you're happy, gently warm the remaining jam in a small saucepan, then sieve and brush all over the cake. Knead the marzipan until pliable. Sprinkle a work surface and rolling pin with confectioners' sugar and roll out the marzipan into a circle slightly larger than the top and sides of the cake, about ¼" thick. Lift on to the cake, smoothing all over, and cut away any excess. Let stand overnight to firm up.

Brush the marzipan with the brandy. On a clean, flat surface, knead the remaining white fondant until pliable. Sprinkle a work surface and rolling pin with confectioners' sugar and roll out the fondant in a circle about ¼" thick and slightly larger than the diameter of the cake and sides. Lift with your hands (or loosely wrap around the rolling pin) and place over the marzipan. Gently smooth with your hands and cut away any excess. Again, let stand overnight to harden.

For the trees, roll out the darker green fondant to about ⅜" thick and cut out 1 large and 5 small trees. Repeat with the lighter green, cutting 2 large and 4 smaller trees. Dip their edges into the glitter. With the royal icing, glue half of them on the candy canes. Re-roll the 2 green fondants to ⅛" thick and cut out 1 large and 5 small trees in darker green and 2 large and 4 small trees in light green. Glue these on to the backs of the trees, to hide the join to the candy canes. Push the 'trunks' into the cake, all facing the same way. Break up the sugar cubes and scatter over the surface, then sprinkle with glitter. Twist the ribbon round the cake and attach at the back with the royal icing.

MAKES 40 SLICES

Rich Tamarind Fruit Cake (page 46)

2¾ pounds white fondant
green food coloring paste
10" round cake drum (optional)
⅓ cup apricot jam
2¼ pounds marzipan (see page 138)
confectioners' sugar, for rolling
1 tablespoon brandy or boiled water
1 large red-and-white candy cane, cut into 2½" lengths
2¾" tree cookie cutter
1½" tree cookie cutter
clear edible glitter
¼ cup royal icing, in a parchment paper cone (see page 9)
2–3 sugar cubes
5 yards ⅛" wide red satin ribbon

glacé fruit and nut cake

The most wonderful jewel-like glacé fruits, imported from Provence, appear in specialty grocers around Christmas. I specify which fruits and nuts I used, but please alter this to your preference and use what you can find. This cake is a truly stunning centerpiece for the festive season, and not a plastic reindeer in sight. Please make sure the bay leaves don't get eaten!

Turn the cake over, so that the flat bottom is uppermost. Combine the jam and rum in a small saucepan and bring to a boil. Let cool a little, rub through a sieve and brush half over the top of the cake.

Roll out the marzipan to ½" thick, using a little confectioners' sugar on the work top and rolling pin. Using the pan as a guide, cut out a marzipan square the same size as the cake with a sharp knife. Lay it on top of the cake.

Brush the marzipan with more of the jam mixture and stud the fruits and nuts all over the surface of the cake, pushing them in so they don't fall off. Tuck the bay leaves in amongst them.

Entwine the raffia around the cake and tie with a knot. If it is not to be eaten for a few days, place a strip of parchment paper underneath the raffia to keep the sides of the cake from drying out.

MAKES 20 SLICES

Tropical Fruit Cake without nuts
  on top (page 44)

¼ cup apricot jam
3 tablespoons rum
1¼ pounds store-bought
  marzipan
confectioners' sugar, for rolling
3 glacé pears
1 glacé clementine
3 glacé figs
6 slices glacé orange
12 whole glacé cherries
60 shelled unsalted pistachios
40 pecans
1 sprig of fresh bay leaves
1¾ yards colored raffia

penguin cake

Originally designed as an alternative Christmas cake, there's no reason not to make this at any time. The penguins need to be kept at room temperature and the cake should not be hours out of the refrigerator or it will become difficult to cut, so decorate shortly before you serve it. The penguins can be made a few weeks ahead and stored in a covered cardboard box (not an airtight container as they will sweat).

To make the "snow," add about 2 tablespoons water to the confectioners' sugar and mix until it is thick enough to coat the back of a spoon. Drizzle all over the top of the cake.

Color 9 ounces of fondant black according to the directions on page 11. Leave the remaining fondant white. Divide the royal icing between 3 separate small bowls. Leave 1 bowl of icing white, and color 1 black and the other yellow. Transfer each icing to a small parchment paper cone (see page 9).

For each penguin, make a cone of black fondant (the largest I made were 1 1/2" tall and the smallest 1"). Snip out 2 wings with the tip of a pair of scissors, and ease them away from the body. Roll out a little ball of white fondant with your fingers, squash it flat to form the tummy and press on to the penguin, adhering with a little white royal icing. Pipe 2 little eyes in white, allow to dry for an hour or so, then pipe in the black centers. Finish by piping a yellow beak. Make snowballs by rolling different-sized balls of white fondant.

Decorate the cake by placing the penguins over and around it, adding the snowballs and, finally, the glitter for sparkle.

SERVES 12

Surprise Icebox Cake (page 56)

1½ cups confectioners' sugar
11 ounces fondant
black food coloring paste
9 tablespoons royal icing
yellow food coloring paste
clear edible glitter

gingerbread man cake

A great classic Christmas cake for all the family; there's always someone who doesn't like fruit cake, so they can eat the gingerbread men!

Two days before serving, turn the cake upside down on to a cake stand. A dab of apricot jam will stop it moving around. If there are any holes or the cake is a dodgy shape, correct it now with little bits of marzipan. Brush all over with jam. Knead the marzipan until pliable. Sprinkle a work surface and rolling pin with confectioners' sugar. Roll the marzipan into a rough circle slightly larger than the top and sides of the cake and about 1/4" thick. Lift on to the cake, smoothing all over, and cut off any excess. Let stand overnight.

Brush the marzipan with the brandy. Repeat the rolling procedure with the fondant to make a double-thick coating over the cake. Gently smooth with your hands and cut away any excess. Let stand overnight to harden.

Preheat the oven to 350°F. Roll the gingerbread dough out to 1/4" thick and cut out 12 large and 12 small men. Line 2 baking sheets with parchment paper. Place the smaller cookies on 1 tray (they take less time to bake) and the larger ones on the other. Press 2 wooden toothpicks on to the backs of the legs of 3 smaller men so they will stand up later. Bake for 8–15 minutes, depending on size. The gingerbread will darken. Cool on a wire rack.

Divide the icing between 3 small bowls. Leave 1 bowl of icing white and color 1 bowl black and the other red. Transfer each to a disposable pastry bag and snip off the tips. Pipe black eyes and red mouths on the large men and stick on red candy noses. Pipe black eyes and red noses and mouths on the small cookies. Stick 3 buttons on the large men and 2 on the small ones. Surround the cake with the larger men, propped against it, dabbing their heads with a little white royal icing to adhere. Carefully position the 3 men on sticks on the top of the cake. You will have 9 little men leftover to serve separately.

MAKES 40 SLICES

Rich Tamarind Fruit Cake
  (page 46)
1/2 batch Gingerbread dough
  (page 73)

1/3 cup apricot jam, warmed and
  sieved
2 1/4 pounds marzipan (see page
  138)
1 tablespoon brandy or boiled
  water
confectioners' sugar, for rolling
2 1/4 pounds white fondant
3 1/2" and 2 1/2" gingerbread man
  cookie cutters
6 wooden toothpicks
1 cup royal icing (see page 9)
black food coloring paste
red food coloring paste
bag of mini sugar-coated
  chocolate candies

marzipan criss-cross

Perfect with a cup of tea on a winter's day.

Place the cake upside down on to a cake stand or serving plate. Warm the jam gently in a small saucepan, run through a sieve, then brush over the top of the cake. On a clean work top sprinkled with confectioners' sugar, roll out the marzipan to ½" thick and the exact size of the top of the cake, using the pan as a guide. Trim the edges with a sharp knife, then lift the marzipan on to the cake. With the back of a long knife, indent the top, making the first indent exactly from one corner to the other and then marking parallel lines either side, each about 2 ½" apart. Repeat in the other direction to form a criss-cross. Wherever the lines meet, press a gold dragee into the marzipan.

To gild the 4 walnuts, mix the alcohol with the gold powder using the brush and paint the walnuts. Place them firmly at each corner of the cake (you may need royal icing to hold them in place). Entwine the raffia around the cake and tie with a knot. If it is not to be eaten for a few days, place a strip of parchment paper underneath the raffia to keep the sides of the cake from drying out.

SERVES 15

Whisky, Date, and Walnut Cake (page 49), baked in a square pan

3 tablespoons apricot jam
confectioners' sugar, for rolling
1¼ pounds marzipan (see recipe below, or use store-bought)
about 50 gold dragees
4 walnut halves
½ teaspoon vodka or gin
edible gold powder
small paint brush
a very little royal icing (optional)
1¾ yards natural raffia

marzipan

MAKES ABOUT 1½ POUNDS, ENOUGH TO COVER AN 8" CAKE

In a bowl, mix the confectioners' sugar and almond flour. In another bowl, mix the lemon juice, egg yolks and almond extract. Add the egg mixture gradually to the almond mixture and knead everything just until it forms a stiff paste. (It will become oily if overworked.) Store in a plastic bag in the refrigerator (use within a week). Many people will prefer to use store-bought marzipan, which can be bought in bulk (see suppliers list, page 207).

1⅔ cups confectioners' sugar, sifted
3⅔ cups almond flour
1 tablespoon fresh lemon juice
3 large egg yolks
4 drops pure almond extract

vintage glamour wedding cake

A beautiful three-tiered timeless classic, this could take center stage at any wedding feast. It can be baked and decorated at least a month in advance and there are no colors to mix as the entire scheme is in ivory fondant with highlights of gold. (You could also make this cake in white and gold.) If you break down each stage, giving yourself plenty of time, you may find it easier than you think.

the nuts and bolts

Thin cake boards are used only while you are assembling the cakes, and really serve to save your work surfaces. You can use any board you have, even plywood. Thick cake drums are used to support each tier of the finished cake, so must be bought for the purpose.

Prepare the cake pans and batter. Divide the batter between the pans, filling each to the same depth. Bake as instructed on page 46. The smallest cake will take about 1³/₄ hours, the medium 2¹/₂–3 hours and the largest about 3 hours: if a wooden toothpick inserted into the center comes out clean, it is ready. Let cool in the pans. When cooled, pierce all over with a fine wooden skewer and sprinkle with the brandy. Wrap in fresh parchment paper, then aluminum foil, until ready to use. You can continue to feed the cakes with 1–2 tablespoons brandy every other week, for a month or two.

to marzipan the cakes

Take the 8" thin board and place the 6" drum on it. Brush 1 tablespoon apricot jam into the center, then place the 6" cake on top, upside down so the flat bottom forms the surface. If it is slightly smaller than the drum, make a strip of marzipan as wide as the side of the cake and the same circumference, and stick it to the edge. Similarly, all cakes should be the same height. If not, apply an extra-thin marzipan layer to the top of the shallow cake (use the pan as a guide). Repeat for the other cakes, placing the 8" cake on the same-size drum and 10" board, and the 10" cake on the same-size drum and 12" board.

Brush the 6" cake with jam. Knead 1³/₄ pounds of marzipan until pliable. Sprinkle a work surface and rolling pin with confectioners' sugar, and roll out into a rough square slightly larger than the top and sides of the cake and drum and about ¹/₄" thick. Lift on to the cake and drum, smooth all over and cut away any excess. Cover the other 2 cakes, using 2¹/₄ pounds marzipan each. Leave overnight to firm up.

SERVES ABOUT 120–150

FOR THE CAKES
one 6" square (3" deep) square
   cake pan
one 8" square (3" deep) square
   cake pan
one 10" square (3" deep) square
   cake pan
2 recipes Rich Tamarind Fruit
   Cake batter (page 46)
6 tablespoons brandy, plus more
   to feed the cake
1 cup apricot jam, gently warmed
   and pushed through a sieve
6³/₄ pounds marzipan (see page
   138)
confectioners' sugar, for rolling

FOR THE BOARDS AND DRUMS
one 8" square thin board
one 10" square thin board
one 12" square thin board
one 6" square (¹/₂" thick) cake
   drum
one 8" square (¹/₂" thick) cake
   drum
one 10" square (¹/₂" thick) cake
   drum

assembly

to cover the base drum

Dust the 12" drum with confectioners' sugar and sprinkle with a small amount of water. Knead 2 1/4 pounds of the fondant until pliable, then sprinkle a work surface and rolling pin with confectioners' sugar and roll it into a rough square slightly larger than the top of the drum and about 1/8" thick. Wrap it loosely around the rolling pin and lift on to the drum. Smooth with your hands and trim away any excess. Replace the excess in a plastic bag and seal. Let dry overnight.

to cover the cakes

The 6" cake will need about 1 3/4 pounds of fondant, and the 2 larger cakes about 2 1/4 pounds each. Work on just 1 cake at a time. For each cake, brush brandy all over the marzipan. This helps the fondant to stick and is an antiseptic. Lightly dust a clean surface with confectioners' sugar and roll out the fondant into a rough square about 1/4" thick and slightly larger than the diameter of the cakes, their sides, and the drums.

Lift the fondant with your hands, place it over the cake and gently smooth, covering the cake and drum. Do not stretch, and work as quickly as you can, before it dries. Cut away any excess, provided it is still clean, and seal in a plastic bag. Let the 3 cakes stand overnight.

to build the cake

Spread 1–2 tablespoons royal icing into the center of the base drum. Gently ease away the largest cake and drum from its board using an icing spatula and place it exactly in the middle of the base drum.

Now insert 4 dowels into the large cake, spacing them to form the corners of a square just within where the 8" cake will sit. Push down each stick until it hits the drum, and mark with a pen about 1/8" above the surface. Remove each stick, score with a knife at the mark, snap (or saw) and discard the excess. Replace each in its hole.

Spread a spoonful of royal icing into the center of the largest cake, remove the 8" cake and drum from its thin board and center on top of the larger cake, resting the drum on the hidden dowels. Repeat the dowel placing process with this middle tier to add the top cake, again using a spoonful of royal icing to keep it steady.

FOR THE CONSTRUCTION
12" square (1/2" thick) cake drum
8 wooden dowels

FOR COVERING THE CAKES
confectioners' sugar, for rolling
9 pounds ivory fondant
2 tablespoons brandy or boiled water
2/3 cup royal icing in a parchment paper cone (see page 9)

decoration

to make the butterflies and blossoms

You will need about 12–15 butterflies and about 100 blossoms in 3 sizes (I made 25 tiny $1/4$" blossoms, 25 medium $1/2$" blossoms and 50 large $5/8$" blossoms).

The decorations are applied randomly, so this is just a guide. Knead some of the fondant left over from covering the cakes and drums until pliable, and roll out thinly (no more than $1/8$" thick) on a board sprinkled with a little confectioners' sugar. Stamp out the blossoms and butterflies and allow to dry for a few hours, preferably overnight. I lay them out as I make them in boxes interleaved with parchment paper. Prop up the butterflies' wings between two sticks (you could use spare dowels), so the wings will dry as if in flight.

If you like, pipe the centers of the blossoms with a tiny dot of royal icing and then press on a gold dragee. If you prefer, just pipe a dot for the centers. Once the butterflies are dry, paint the edges of the wings with egg white and dip into the glitter.

To finish the cake, apply the ribbons by sticking them at the back of each cake using a little royal icing. On the middle tier, overlay the wide organza ribbon with 2 bands of narrow gold ribbon. Wrap the base drum with the double-sided sticky tape, then stick on its ribbon.

Casual, informal designs do have one huge advantage: any blemishes or marks in the icing can be covered by a decoration! Randomly apply the butterflies and little blossoms all over the 3-tiered cake, sticking on with the royal icing. As a final touch, place the 2 doves in the center of the top tier.

FOR THE ADORNMENTS

confectioners' sugar, for rolling
set of 3 blossom plunger cutters
  ($1/4$", $1/2$", and $5/8$")
$1 1/4$" butterfly cutter
2 tablespoons royal icing in a
  parchment paper cone (see
  page 9)
100 small gold dragees in 2 sizes
  (optional); I used 50 medium
  and 50 small gold dragees
1 small paint brush
1 large egg white, lightly beaten
  (or 2 teaspoons dried egg white
  mixed with water until frothy)
edible gold glitter
2 small artificial ivory or white
  doves (or other birds)

FOR THE TOP TIER
two feet $1 1/2$" wide vintage
  gold ribbon

FOR THE MIDDLE TIER
one yard $1 1/2$" wide cream
  organza
$6 1/4$ feet $1/4$" wide gold ribbon

FOR THE BOTTOM TIER
4 feet $2 1/2$" wide gold bejewelled
  ribbon

FOR THE BASE DRUM
1 roll double-sided sticky tape
about $4 1/2$ feet $1/2$" wide ivory
  ribbon

chocolate spiral

I love this unusual cone-shaped cake. I know someone who once used a traffic cone to make it...not to be encouraged! It is very easy, though fairly messy. Try to make this in the cooler months, when working with chocolate and making chocolate leaves is so much easier.

Make the cone. The center of the long side of the cardboard is to be its tip. Twist the cardboard around, tape very firmly into place and cut the base flat; your cone should be about 14" high and 8" in diameter. Very lightly butter the inside and line with plastic wrap. Stand it upside down in a suitable stable container, such as a large vase.

Now cut out rounds of cake with a sharp knife, using cutters, mugs, saucers or small cans as guides. Place the smallest disk in the tip of the mold, then spread with icing. Layer in more disks, getting ever bigger and spreading icing in between. Fill in gaps with pieces of cake and finish with a large cake as the base. Refrigerate overnight to set.

Carefully invert the cone on to its final serving plate or stand. Remove the cardboard and plastic wrap. Make a tip with the fondant or marzipan and, with a little icing, stick it on top. Spread the remaining icing all around the cake, filling in gaps and smoothing the sides.

To make the chocolate leaves, place a small heatproof bowl over a saucepan of gently simmering water, making sure the bottom of the bowl does not touch the water. Add the chocolate and heat until melted, stirring only very occasionally. Dip the undersides of the leaves into the chocolate. Place, chocolate-side up, on a tray lined with parchment paper, propped up on bits of rolled-up aluminum foil so they don't lie completely flat. Let the chocolate set in the refrigerator. Gently peel off the real leaves, holding the stems. You may break a few (I do!) so make more than you need. (I used 60 on this cake.) Stick the leaves on to the iced cone in a spiral. Overlap the leaves and, if any edges are slightly broken, hide them behind another overlapping leaf. Finish with the gold dragees.

SERVES 25–30

2 recipes Family Chocolate Cake (page 17)
2 recipes Fudge Icing (page 17)

one 30 x 40" craft cardboard
strong cellophane tape
butter, for the mold
1½ ounces fondant or marzipan
3½ ounces bittersweet chocolate (70% cacao), chopped
60–70 mint or rose leaves with prominent veins, washed and dried thoroughly
about 60 gold dragees

tiered marie antoinette's cake

Whether she did or didn't actually say "let them eat cake," I choose to think that she did! Inspired by the exquisite costumes and dazzling confections of the French court at the Palace of Versailles, this beautiful cake is fit for a queen, with its adornments of ostrich feathers, pearls, ribbons, and rosebuds. Ideal for a wedding or special birthday party.

MAKES 80 SMALL PIECES

the nuts and bolts

You can both make and freeze the unadorned cakes and prepare the lavender sugar a month in advance if you want to get ahead. Thin cake boards are only to assemble the cakes, so use any board you have. Cake drums support each tier, so must be bought for the purpose.

You need to make 3 cakes, as the 2 larger cakes, sandwiched together, form the bottom tier. Follow the instructions for making the Orange Drizzle Cake (page 32), baking the 1 smaller, deeper cake for 40–45 minutes and the 2 larger, shallower cakes for just 35–40 minutes.

Tip the confectioners' sugar into a food processor and add the lavender. Process until very fine. Store in a sealed container for a week to allow the flavor to develop. Sift and store in an airtight container.

to buttercream the cakes
In an electric mixer, cream the butter and lemon zest for 1–2 minutes until fluffy, then add half the lavender sugar. Mix for 5 minutes, then add the remaining sugar and the juice and mix for 1–2 minutes. Trim the tops of all 3 cakes with a serrated knife just until level. The cakes should be about the same height once filled, so fill the smaller cake with more buttercream than the larger, and fill in any holes or cracks.

Slice the smaller cake in half and place the top half upside down on to the 8" drum, securing with buttercream. Place on the smaller thin board. Spread buttercream on the cut surface, then top with the inverted other half. For the larger cake, place 1 cake on the 10" cake drum, again securing with buttercream, and lift on to the 12" thin board. Spread with buttercream, then top with the second cake, inverted so its bottom forms the top. Smooth the remaining buttercream over the top and sides of both.

FOR THE CAKES
one 8 x 3" round cake pan
two 10 x 3" round cake pans
3 recipes Orange Drizzle Cake batter (page 32), with the orange zest and juice replaced by lemon zest and juice

FOR THE LAVENDER SUGAR
2¾ cups confectioners' sugar, sifted
¼ cup dried culinary lavender

FOR THE BUTTERCREAM
2 cups unsalted butter, softened
finely grated zest of 2 organic lemons
juice of 1 organic lemon

FOR THE BOARDS AND DRUMS
one 8 x ½" round cake drum
one 10 x ½" round cake drum
one 12 x ½" round cake drum
one 8" round thin board
one 12" round thin board

assembly

to color the fondant

Cut off 3½ ounces of the fondant and place it in a sealed plastic bag at room temperature. This will make the roses and rosebuds. Color the remaining fondant with the food coloring paste (see page 11), aiming for the pale pink shown on page 149. Divide into thirds, 1 part for the base drum and 1 part for each cake. Place into separate plastic food bags and seal. Let stand overnight at room temperature.

to cover the base drum

Sprinkle the 12" drum with confectioners' sugar and then a little water. Knead a third of the pink fondant until pliable, then, on a surface lightly sprinkled with confectioners' sugar, roll into a circle slightly larger than the top of the drum and about ⅛" thick. Wrap it loosely around the rolling pin and lift on to the drum. Smooth with your hands. Trim away any excess overhanging the sides and reseal the trimmings in the bag. Let stand at room temperature overnight.

to cover the cakes

Lightly sprinkle a clean, flat surface with confectioners' sugar. Roll out both the remaining pink fondant blocks, one at a time, into circles about ¼" thick and slightly larger than the diameter of each cake, its sides and drum. Wrap each circle loosely around the rolling pin, place it over the cake and gently smooth with your hands. Do not stretch the fondant, and work quickly, as it will dry out. Cut away any excess at the foot of the drums and reseal it in the bag. Take a large knife and roll it gently along the top surface of the cakes, scoring lines to form a criss-cross (each line about ¾" apart) to resemble quilting. Push a dragee in where the lines meet. The center of the bottom tier will not be seen, so no need to use dragees. Let stand overnight.

to build the cake

Spread 3-4 tablespoons of royal icing into the center of the base drum. Ease the larger cake and drum from its thin board with an icing spatula, and place it in the exact center of the base drum. Now insert the dowels vertically into the cake, spacing them out to form the corners of a square just within where the smaller cake will sit. Push down each stick until it hits the drum, and mark with a pen about ⅛" above the surface. Remove each stick, score with a knife at the mark, then snap (or saw) and discard the excess. Replace each in its hole. Spread 3-4 tablespoons royal icing into the center of the larger cake, remove the smaller cake and drum from its thin board and place on top, resting the drum on the dowels and using the royal icing as 'glue.'

FOR THE SUGARPASTE
6½ pounds white fondant
burgundy food coloring paste

FOR THE CONSTRUCTION
confectioners' sugar, for rolling
about 200 silver dragees
½ cup white royal icing (see page 9)
4 wooden dowels

decoration

No cutters are required for this cake and, if piping swags seems too difficult, just pipe simple dots around the edges. Fresh flowers could be used on top instead of the fondant roses, if you prefer. You should find a good supply of beading, braids, and feathers in a crafts store.

to make the roses and rosebuds

Turn to the reserved white fondant. Tint about $1^1/2$ ounces of it green and 2 ounces off-white, using a tiny amount of olive green and a pinprick of ivory pastes respectively (see page 11). Tint about $10^1/2$ ounces of the pink fondant reserved from covering the cake a deeper pink, using more burgundy paste. Reseal all colors in separate plastic bags.

Make a few rosebuds at a time. On a board sprinkled with confectioners' sugar, roll out a little of the deeper pink fondant to $1/8$" thick. Cut into strips of 4 x $5/8$" and roll each into little buds. Cut away surplus at the base. Repeat to make 16 rosebuds. Make the leaves with the green fondant. Take a little ball at a time and shape into a tiny leaf. Score with a knife to resemble the central vein. Make 3 large leaves and pinch to make the veins. Dip into glitter. Let the rosebuds and leaves dry, preferably overnight.

To make the larger roses, see page 129, forming one each from ivory, light pink and deep pink sugarpaste. When dry, paint the edges of the petals with egg white, dip into the glitter, then shake off excess.

the finishing touches

Apply all the ribbons, braids and beading by sticking them at the back of the cake using a little royal icing. Use the double-sided tape to stick the braid to the side of the base drum. Stick on the rosebuds and leaves with royal icing, spacing them out about 3" apart on the top tier and 4" apart on the bottom tier. Each tier will have 8 rosebuds.

Push the flower pick into the center of the cake. Stand the ostrich feather and pearl spray in the pick, using a little fondant inside the tube to support it if necessary. Use the royal icing to adhere the 3 large roses and leaves around the base of the feather.

Finish the cake by piping half-circle swags between the rosebuds, then dots. This is easier if you gently tilt the cake up towards you by placing a book under the board. Simple tiny randomly piped dots, about 1" apart, all over the sides will look just as effective.

FOR THE ROSES AND ROSEBUDS
olive green food coloring paste
ivory food coloring paste
1 large egg white, lightly beaten (or 2 teaspoons dried egg white mixed with water until frothy)
clear edible glitter
$1/4$ cup royal icing in a small disposable pastry bag fitted with a $1/8$" plain tip

FOR THE BASE DRUM
40 inches $3/4$" wide braid or ribbon
double-sided sticky tape

FOR THE BOTTOM TIER
1 yard pale pink satin ribbon
1 yard thinner braided ribbon, ideally in pink and pale green

FOR THE TOP TIER
28" pale cream and pink ribbon
28" pearl beading
1 floral water pick, or small plastic tube from a florist
1 ostrich feather
1 spray of pearls on wires

cupcakes

butterfly cakes

The straightforward flavors in these individual cakes are universally popular.

Preheat the oven to 350°F.

Line 18 muffin cups in 2 pans with paper liners and divide the batter evenly between them. Bake for about 20 minutes, or until the cakes are well risen and spring back to the touch. Leave in the pans for 1–2 minutes. Remove and cool completely on a wire rack.

For the vanilla buttercream, cream the butter until pale and fluffy. Add the vanilla and then the confectioners' sugar. Beat for about 5 minutes until really light. Make the chocolate buttercream in the same way, adding the cocoa powder with the confectioners' sugar and omitting the vanilla.

To make the wings, cut out a shallow cone from the top of each cake and cut the cone in half. Spoon a swirl of buttercream into the cut-out dip on top of each cake and place the wings back in at an angle. Sift confectioners' sugar on top and arrange on a cake stand or plate.

MAKES 18

Victoria Sponge Cake batter
  (page 24)

18 paper cupcake liners
confectioners' sugar, for garnish

FOR VANILLA BUTTERCREAM
14 tablespoons unsalted butter,
  softened
1 teaspoon vanilla extract
2¼ cups confectioners' sugar,
  sifted

FOR CHOCOLATE BUTTERCREAM
14 tablespoons unsalted butter,
  softened
½ cup cocoa powder
2 cups confectioners' sugar, sifted

garland cakes

These exquisitely intricate paper wrappers embellish the cupcakes, which are very simply iced and decorated. You can create an impressive display with very little effort and you should be able to reuse the wrappers. They are readily available at cake decorating shops and online (see suppliers, page 207). I added 1½ teaspoons of very tiny dragees for this photo, but you can use all the same size if it's easier.

Preheat the oven to 350°F.

Line 12 muffin cups with foil liners and divide the batter evenly between them. Bake for about 20 minutes, or until the cakes are well risen and spring back to the touch. Let cool in the pans for 1–2 minutes. Remove and cool on a wire rack.

Make the topping by creaming the confectioners' sugar, butter, and zest for about 5 minutes until pale and fluffy, then add the mascarpone, vanilla, and Cointreau (do not overmix as it may become too liquid). Pipe the buttercream on to each cake using the pastry bag fitted with the large star tip. Sprinkle the silver dragees on to the cakes in silver cases, and the gold dragees on to the cakes in gold cases.

When ready to serve, assemble the 12 paper wrappers, place a cake in each one and serve.

MAKES 12

Victoria Sponge Cake batter
  (page 24)

6 silver foil cupcake liners
6 gold foil cupcake liners
1 cup confectioners' sugar, sifted
7 tablespoons unsalted butter,
  softened
finely grated zest of 2 organic
  oranges
17 ounces mascarpone
1 teaspoon vanilla extract
1 tablespoon Cointreau (optional)
pastry bag fitted with a large star
  pastry tip
1 tablespoon silver and gold
  dragees
12 cupcake wrappers

rosebud cupcakes

A cake stand piled with these enchanting creations in pastel pinks would be lovely for a girlie afternoon tea or birthday party. Make more for a larger celebration or even a wedding. The rosebuds can be made a month or two in advance; store in a cardboard box at room temperature.

Preheat the oven to 350°F. Line 24 mini muffin cups with paper liners and divide the batter evenly between them. Bake for about 15 minutes or until well risen and the cakes spring back to the touch. Let cool in the pans for 1–2 minutes. Remove and cool on a wire rack.

Make the buttercream: cream the butter until pale and fluffy, add the rose water, if desired, and the vanilla. Beat in the confectioners' sugar for about 5 minutes until very light, adding enough food coloring paste to achieve the shade of pink you want. Divide between all the cakes, spreading with an icing spatula.

To make the rosebuds, divide the fondant in thirds and color each a different shade of pink (start with the darkest pink, see page 11). Seal in separate plastic bags. Sprinkle a work surface and rolling pin with confectioners' sugar. Roll out a little of the fondant to about 1/8" thick. Cut 3 or 4 strips about 4 x 5/8" and roll them up to form rosebuds. Cut away any surplus at the base. Repeat to make 24 buds, 8 in each tone of pink. Place 1 on each cake.

Tint the royal icing green and transfer to a parchment paper cone (see page 9). Snip the tip of the pastry bag in a V-shape (the "V" should point towards the bag). Pipe a leaf or 2 on each cake, or leave some without if you prefer. Scatter glitter over the cakes, if you wish.

MAKES 24

Victoria Sponge Cake batter
  (page 24)

24 mini cupcake paper liners
14 tablespoons unsalted butter,
  softened
1 teaspoon rose water (optional)
1 teaspoon vanilla extract
2¼ cups confectioners' sugar,
  plus more for garnish
pink food coloring paste
3 ounces white fondant
¼ cup royal icing (see page 9)
green food coloring paste
clear glitter (optional)

crystallized flower cupcakes

Perfect for any garden party, these are as pretty as a picture. In this recipe, they are iced in very pale lavender and green pastels to complement the flowers used, but you can use any colors of your choice. For a large party or wedding, a stand of these on each table would make a fabulous centerpiece.

Preheat the oven to 350°F.

Line 22 muffin cups in 2 muffin pans with paper liners and divide the batter evenly between them (make sure each is only just over half full, as you need space to spread the icing). Bake for 15 minutes, or until the cakes are well risen and spring back to the touch. Leave for 1–2 minutes in the pans. Remove to a wire rack and cool.

Divide the confectioners' sugar between 2 bowls. Very gradually add a little orange juice to each until it is thick enough to coat the back of a spoon. Add a very little purple food coloring to one bowl and blend it in well until you achieve the desired shade. Cover the bowl with plastic wrap (the icing dries out very quickly) while you color the other icing in the same way, using the green food coloring.

To ice the cakes, replace them in the muffin pan. This makes it much easier as the cups will hold the shapes of the cakes. Spread enough icing on to the cakes - using each color on about half the batch - so that it is almost level with the top of the liner, gently easing it to the edges with the back of a spoon. Allow to dry for a couple of hours. The cakes can be iced 2 days ahead, but add the flowers on the day they are to be eaten.

To finish, arrange the crystallized flowers and leaves on the cakes, using dabs of royal icing to hold them in place. Display on cake stands or plates, scattering any remaining flowers and leaves in between.

MAKES ABOUT 22

Orange Drizzle Cake batter (page 32)

22 paper cupcake liners
5½ cups confectioners' sugar, sifted
4–8 tablespoons fresh orange juice
purple food coloring paste
green food coloring paste
20–30 edible crystallized flowers and leaves (I used lavender, tiny rosebuds, anchusa, daisies and pinks, and geranium and rosemary leaves, see page 107)
royal icing (see page 9)

ice-cream cones

Ice cream that won't melt! Perfect for any children's party, especially during the summer. These are decorated as the real things – soft-serve vanilla with a chocolate bar, raspberry ripple, or mint chocolate chip – but use your imagination and get the children to help. These cakes are baked in ice-cream cones, so eat them quickly as they dry out after a day or so. That shouldn't prove difficult!

Preheat the oven to 350°F. Place all the ice-cream cones on a baking sheet. Divide the cake batter evenly between them and bake for 15–17 minutes, or until they spring back to the touch. Let cool on a wire rack.

Divide the buttercream between 3 bowls. Add a little peppermint extract to the first, to taste, then a dash of green food coloring, and mix until you achieve the desired shade. Add the vanilla to the second bowl and mix well. To the third bowl, swirl in a little pink food coloring; do not blend it in as you are aiming for the marbled effect of raspberry ripple ice cream.

Spoon the vanilla buttercream into the pastry bag fitted with the star tip and swirl on to a third of the ice-cream cones. Finish each with a chocolate bar. Wash the bag and tip and repeat with the green buttercream, sprinkling with chocolate chips. Wash the bag and tip again. Finally pipe the raspberry ripple buttercream into the remaining cones and decorate with sprinkles.

Arrange on a serving dish or cake stand.

MAKES 20–25

Orange Drizzle Cake batter
  (page 32)

20–25 flat-bottomed ice-cream
  cones
Buttercream (see page 9)
few drops of peppermint extract
green food coloring
1 teaspoon vanilla extract
pink (or red) food coloring
pastry bag fitted with a large star
  pastry tip
7–8 chocolate bars (optional)
7 teaspoons mini chocolate chips
5 teaspoons colored sugar
  sprinkles

fondant petits fours

From a very young age, the cakes my children wanted to eat were icing-covered, pastel-colored petits fours from our local supermarket bakery. Every cake I made was up for comparison and rarely equalled them; never surpassing! Here are my petits fours with a contemporary twist, iced in 4 colors. You could easily use fewer colors; choose whichever appeal to you.

Preheat the oven to 350°F. Butter an 8" square (3" deep) cake pan and line the bottom with parchment paper. Spread the batter in the pan. Bake for about 35 minutes, or until a wooden toothpick inserted into the center of the cake comes out clean. Let stand for a few minutes. Turn out on to a wire rack and cool.

Make the buttercream using the butter, a scant 1 cup of the confectioners' sugar and the vanilla (see page 9). Split the cake horizontally, and fill with buttercream. Refrigerate or freeze to firm up for about 1 hour.

Meanwhile prepare the glacé icing. Place the remaining confectioners' sugar into a large bowl. Gradually add water until the icing is thick enough to coat the back of a spoon. Keep it fairly stiff, as the food colorings will thin the icing. You can always add water later.

Divide into 4 bowls. Blend burgundy food coloring into the first to make a pale pink; olive green, ice-blue, and egg yellow to another for the green; egg yellow and a pin prick of burgundy to the third for yellow; violet and a little burgundy to the last for purple. Cover all the bowls with plastic wrap so the icing doesn't dry out.

Take the cake out of the refrigerator or freezer and, with a sharp knife, cut into 25 little squares. Turn each upside down so its flat bottom forms the top surface. Take 6 and place on a wire rack. Spoon over 1 color of the glacé icing, easing it down the sides with the back of a teaspoon. While still wet, decorate with your chosen decorations: tiny sugar flowers, dragees, or angelica. Use leftover glacé icing in a contrasting color to decorate: place a little into a pastry bag, snip off the end and pipe in a zigzag fashion over the top of some of the cakes. Repeat with another 6 cakes and another color, until all are iced.

MAKES 25

Victoria Sponge batter
  (page 24)

7 tablespoons unsalted butter, softened, plus more for the pan
3 pounds (about 12¾ cups) confectioners' sugar, sifted
1 teaspoon vanilla extract
burgundy, olive green, ice-blue, egg yellow, and violet food coloring pastes
selection of tiny sugar flowers, dragees and angelica
2 disposable pastry bags

mint cupcakes

I love the contrast between chocolate cake and this pale mint buttercream. Be careful, when buying the mint chocolate, to avoid a bar with a creme center! Naturally, the chocolate itself should contain the mint flavor. If you can't find it, use bittersweet chocolate and ½ teaspoon peppermint extract.

Preheat the oven to 350°F.

Line 16–18 muffin cups with the paper liners. Divide the batter between them. Bake for 25–30 minutes. When they spring back to the touch, transfer to a wire rack and cool completely.

Meanwhile, beat together the butter and confectioners' sugar for a good 5 minutes until really light. Beat in the peppermint extract and a touch of green food coloring.

With an icing spatula, spread buttercream on to the cupcakes and decorate each with a sprig of mint.

MAKES 16–18

Family Chocolate Cake batter, made with mint dark chocolate (page 17)

18 paper cupcake liners
14 tablespoons unsalted butter, softened
2¼ cups confectioners' sugar, sifted
few drops of peppermint extract, to taste
green food coloring paste
18 sprigs fresh or crystallized mint leaves (page 107)

chile chocolate cupcakes

Chile-flavored chocolate is used for this lovely, shiny icing
and each cake is decorated with a whole chile...munch on
it at your peril! Don't worry about the heat of the chocolate
icing itself, though, as it only has a mild kick. I also give
recipes for a chocolate-vanilla and a chocolate-mocha icing
here, in case chile peppers aren't for you.

Preheat the oven to 350°F. Line 15 muffin cups, in 2 muffin pans, with
the paper liners. Divide the batter evenly between them. Bake for 17–
20 minutes, or until the cakes spring back to the touch. Don't worry
if they crack in the oven; the icing will cover any fissures. Transfer to a
wire rack and cool completely.

Meanwhile, make the icing. In a heavy-bottomed saucepan, combine
7 tablespoons water, the chocolate, sugar, and syrup, and gently bring
to a boil, stirring so it doesn't scorch on the bottom of the pan. Stir
constantly for about 3 minutes, or until thickened. Remove from
the heat and stir in the butter.

Let cool. Spoon over the cupcakes. If the icing thickens too much
before you have finished coating the cakes, simply reheat it very
gently. Place a chile on each cupcake as you apply the icing. Let cool
and set completely.

other icing flavorings

chocolate-vanilla use unflavored bittersweet chocolate and add
1 teaspoon vanilla extract with the butter

chocolate-mocha use unflavored bittersweet chocolate and
replace the water with strong brewed coffee.

MAKES 15

½ recipe Chocolate Celebration
   Cake batter (page 14)

15 paper cupcake liners
5½ ounces chile-flavored
   bittersweet chocolate, such
   as Lindt, finely chopped
⅓ cup granulated sugar
2 tablespoons golden syrup
2 tablespoons unsalted butter
15 fresh red chile peppers

daisy and sunflower cupcakes

The current vogue for cupcakes started in New York bakeries. I took a trip there recently and was fascinated by all the vibrant colors. These are inspired by those Manhattan creations. The buttercream here is beautifully mellow rather than very sweet, which is deliberate. Do try it, as it complements the Carrot-Pecan cakes wonderfully.

Preheat the oven to 325°F.

Line 12 muffin cups with the paper liners. Divide the batter between them. Bake for 25–30 minutes or until they spring back to the touch. Let cool in the pan for a minute or 2, then transfer to a wire rack.

Meanwhile make the topping. Beat the confectioners' sugar, butter, maple syrup, and zest until really light and fluffy, about 5 minutes. In a separate bowl beat the cream cheese until smooth, then fold into the butter mixture; do not over-mix as it may become too loose to pipe. If it is too soft, chill for an hour to firm it up. Divide into 2 bowls and color the first a pale sunflower yellow, adding more confectioners' sugar if it becomes too liquid.

Fill 1 pastry bag with yellow icing and the other with plain. Snip a V shape into each end (with the point of the "V" facing the bag) and pipe petals on to each cake. Pipe a little icing into the center and fill with the candies; yellow for daisies and brown for sunflowers.

MAKES 12

Carrot-Pecan Cake batter
  (Page 43)

12 paper cupcake liners
2/3 cup confectioners' sugar, sifted
6½ tablespoons unsalted butter,
  softened
1 tablespoon maple syrup
finely grated zest of 1 organic
  orange
5½ ounces cream cheese,
  softened
yellow food coloring paste
2 disposable pastry bags
96 yellow mini sugar-coated
  chocolate candies
96 brown mini sugar-coated
  chocolate candies

parcels

We all love to receive a beautifully wrapped gift and these edible parcels are a delight. Children will love to decorate them, and the possibilities are endless (see page 202). You could decorate a large cake instead of quarters, if you prefer.

Preheat the oven to 350°F. Butter a 9" square cake pan and line the bottom with parchment paper. Spread the batter in the pan. Bake for 40–50 minutes, or until a wooden toothpick inserted into the center comes out clean. Cool completely.

Refrigerate the cake for an hour or 2. It will be easier to cut when chilled. Turn it upside down, split it and sandwich with some of the fudge icing. Trim the sides, then cut the cake into 4 equal squares. Place on the boards, adhering with a dab of fudge icing in the center. Spread a little fudge icing over the top and sides of each. Great care needs to be taken here not to spread it right down to the board; stop about 1/2" above it otherwise the fudge icing will soil the fondant.

Separate the fondant into 4 portions. Sprinkle a work surface and your rolling pin with confectioners' sugar, then roll out 1 piece at a time to a square about 1/4" thick and slightly larger than the top and sides of the cake. Lift on to a cake, smooth with your hands, then cut away the excess. Repeat with the other 3 cakes.

Make 'paper folds' with the blunt side of a knife on 2 opposite ends of each parcel. Secure a piece of ribbon at the opposite bases of each parcel using royal icing and repeat with another ribbon. Do not tuck the ribbons under the cake or they may become stained. Tie a ribbon bow and stick it, with a tassel, in the center of each parcel. Finally, decorate the 'wrapping paper' by glueing on the mini beans.

MAKES 4

Family Chocolate Cake batter
  (page 17)
Fudge Icing (page 17)

butter, for the pan
four 6" square cardboard cake
  boards
2¾ pounds white fondant
confectioners' sugar, for rolling
four 1 yard (⅝" wide) ribbons in
  contrasting colours
¼ cup royal icing in a parchment
  paper cone (see page 9)
4 small tassels
80 mini sugar-coated candies in
  4 colors

fancy hats

Become a milliner and design your own hats in cake and icing. I have created a tall black-and-white hat fit for any wedding, a top hat, a cap, and summer boaters. Take these as a starting point and create your own range of exquisite headgear!

Color 3½ ounces of fondant for the top hat, using the black and violet food coloring pastes (see page 11) and seal in a plastic bag.

Sprinkle all the cake boards with a little confectioners' sugar and a little water. Make the rims of the hats: on a work top lightly sprinkled with confectioners' sugar, and with a sugar-sprinkled rolling pin, roll out some of the white fondant to ⅛" thick. Using the round cutters, cut out two 4" rounds, three 3" rounds, and one 2" round. Place these on their appropriate boards. Roll out a little of the colored fondant to the same thickness, cut out a 3" round and place on the remaining cake board. Spread a little jam into the centre of each board.

Now cut out the Victoria Sponge Cake. These circles of cake will form the hat crowns. Using more of the jam, sandwich together two 2" rounds for the top hat, three 2" rounds for the tallest hat, and two 1¾" rounds for the cap. Cut the top layer of the cap at an angle, with a sharp knife, so the crown slopes backward. Cut out 4 more 2" rounds for the remaining cakes. Brush each with jam.

Next, sprinkling the work surface and rolling pin with a little confectioners' sugar, roll out the remaining white fondant and use it to cover each cake crown (except for the top hat). Cover the top hat with the colored fondant. Smooth each with your hands and, when you are pleased with the shapes, put the cakes on their boards, placing the cap towards the rear of the smallest cake board to make a 'peak.' Run a finger down the centre of one of them to indent. Let dry overnight.

To decorate the hats, use royal icing to attach the ribbons, netting, dragees, feathers, braid, and silk flowers, as desired.

MAKES 7 HATS

Victoria Sponge Cake baked in two 8" layer pans (page 24)

1½ pounds white fondant
black food coloring paste
violet food coloring paste
one 2" diameter round, cut from thin cake cardboard
four 3" diameter rounds, cut from thin cake cardboard
two 4" diameter rounds, cut from thin cake cardboard
confectioners' sugar, for rolling
4", 3", 2", and 1¾" round metal cutters
½ cup apricot jam, warmed and sieved
¼ cup royal icing in a parchment paper cone (see page 9)
selection of ribbons, netting, dragees, feathers, braid, and tiny silk flowers

mini tiered cakes

Tiered cakes don't need to be kept for weddings! Here are miniature cakes, created from a variety of cupcake, mini muffin and ovenproof candy liners. This recipe is very versatile: try it with Family Chocolate Cake (page 17); Victoria Sponge Cake (page 24); Very Lemony Crunch Cake (page 31), or Orange Drizzle Cake (page 32).

Color the fondant using a very little of the food coloring paste (see page 11). Seal in a plastic bag at room temperature until ready to use.

Preheat the oven to 325°F. Line 8 each mini muffin and cupcake cups with the appropriate liners. Stand the candy cases on a baking sheet. Pour in the batter. Bake the smallest for about 15 minutes, the medium-sized for about 20 minutes and the largest for 25–30 minutes, or until each springs back to the touch.

Let cool on a wire rack. Remove each cake from its paper liner. Warm the apricot jam in a small saucepan, sieve and brush all over the top surfaces of the cakes. Roll out the fondant on a work surface lightly sprinkled with confectioners' sugar (sprinkle your rolling pin too) to around 1/4" thick. Cut out 8 disks in each of the 3 sizes and place on top of the cakes, securing with a dab of royal icing. Place a dab of royal icing on a cupcake, put a mini cupcake on top, add another dab of royal icing and top with a tiny cupcake. Repeat until you have made all 8 cakes.

Decorate with 8 dragees on the top tier, 6 little sugar flowers around the middle tier, and about 8 on the bottom, using the royal icing to glue them. Cut eight 8" strips of the thinnest ribbon for the top tier and simply cross over at the front, adhering with a little royal icing at the back. Repeat with the middle and bottom layers using roughly 12" strips of the contrasting 1/4"-wide and 1"-wide ribbon respectively. These cakes can be stored in an airtight container for up to 2 days; no longer, as they will dry out more quickly than usual because their paper cases have been removed.

MAKES 8 CAKES

Carrot-Pecan Cake batter
(page 43)

14 ounces white fondant
violet food coloring paste
8 mini muffin paper liners
8 cupcake paper liners
8 ovenproof foil candy liners
1/4 cup apricot jam
confectioners' sugar, for rolling
1 1/4", 2", and 2 1/2" fluted round
metal cutters
1/4 cup royal icing in a parchment
paper cone (see page 9)
64 colored dragees
112 tiny sugar flowers
64" (1/4" wide) ribbon
96" (1/4" wide) contrasting ribbon
96" (1" wide) ribbon

flying insects

Flying insects and wriggly worms will delight young children, both to make and to eat (especially the worms). The insects can be made a few weeks ahead and must be finished at least the day before, and stored in a cardboard box at room temperature.

Make all the insects at least the day before. Divide the fondant into 5 bowls. Color them red, pink, black and yellow (see page 11). Leave the last one white. Seal in 5 plastic bags at room temperature.

For the ladybirds, roll 8 red balls and shape them to be narrower toward the head. With a knife, make a seam down the middle for the wings. Make a little ball of black and, with black royal icing, attach these heads to the bodies. Pipe 2 eyes with white royal icing, then black dots on to the back. To make the spiders, roll the remaining black fondant into 8 balls, flatten and roll in chocolate sprinkles. For the legs, cut four 2" licorice strands per spider and attach to the underside with black royal icing. Pipe 2 eyes in white.

For the worms, roll 8 sausages of pink fondant – wider at one end for the head – and indent with the knife along the backs. Make the tails by rolling 8 smaller sausages and indent again. Pipe 2 white eyes. To make the bees, shape 8 yellow balls, making the head end a little wider, and pipe 3 black stripes over each body and 2 black eyes. Roll the white fondant out and cut out 16 hearts (or mold 16 ovals) to form wings. Attach with white royal icing.

Preheat the oven to 350°F. Line 24 mini muffin pans with the paper liners (or bake in batches). Pour in the batter and bake for 12–15 minutes. Transfer to a wire rack and let cool completely. Remove from the pans. Ice with the buttercream.

Push a toothpick into each insect. Attach 1 insect to each cake; for the worms, make 2 holes with the end of a teaspoon and push a head and a tail into 8 cakes so the worm seems to be crawling through. Scatter ¼ teaspoon sprinkles on the spider and worm cakes. Arrange 5 red mini candies around the base of each ladybird and 5 pink for the bees.

MAKES 32

Sticky Toffee Cupcakes batter (page 64)

12 ounces white fondant
red food coloring paste
pink food coloring paste
black food coloring paste
yellow food coloring paste
6 tablespoons royal icing (see page 9)
4 teaspoons chocolate sprinkles
8 long black licorice strands
confectioners' sugar, for rolling
¾" heart cutter (optional)
32 mini cupcake paper liners
Vanilla Buttercream (see page 9)
24 wooden toothpicks
2 teaspoons colored sprinkles
40 red miniature sugar-coated chocolate candies
40 pink miniature sugar-coated chocolate candies

fairy tale garden cupcakes

Create an enchanting flower garden just like a child's drawing; perfect for a birthday party. Lollipop 'flowers,' green sugar 'grass' and angelica 'leaves' mean these little orange and lemon cakes take no time at all.

Make the 'grass' by mixing a drop or two of water and the green food coloring together in a small bowl, then add the sugar. Rub together with your fingers until all the sugar has been dyed. Let dry for a few hours. Line 15 cups in 2 muffin pans with the paper liners. Preheat the oven to 350°F.

Divide the batter between the pans. Bake for 20–25 minutes, or until they spring back to the touch. Transfer to a wire rack and cool completely.

Spread the buttercream over the surface of each cake. Sprinkle with the colored green sugar.

Soften the angelica for a minute or so in warm water. Make the leaves by snipping the angelica into narrow strips and then diagonally across into diamonds. Place a lollipop 'flower' into the center of each cake and surround with 2 angelica 'leaves.' Arrange on a cake stand or serving plate, or even under a cloche or among a few flower pots.

MAKES 15

Very Lemony Crunch Cake batter
  (page 31)

green food coloring
¼ cup granulated sugar
15 paper cupcake liners
½ recipe Orange Buttercream
  (see page 9)
2 ounces crystallized angelica
15 flower lollipops

tiny fairy cakes

These little bite-sized cakes are made in petit four cases. The blossoms and butterflies can be made ahead and stored at room temperature in a cardboard box, not in an airtight container or sealed tin. The cakes themselves can be made 2 days ahead, but no longer or they will dry out.

Preheat the oven to 350°F. Place the candy cases on baking sheets. Divide the batter evenly between them. Bake for about 10 minutes, or until the cakes spring back to the touch. Let cool on a wire rack. The shapes may be irregular but that is part of their charm.

Sift the confectioners' sugar into a bowl. Gradually stir in the lemon juice until the mixture thickly coats the back of a spoon. Divide evenly between 3 bowls. Mix a very little blue food coloring into the first bowl to get the desired shade. Cover the bowl with plastic wrap. Repeat the process with the other 2 bowls, using the yellow and pink food colorings.

Pour 1 teaspoon icing on each cake, using each color on about one-third of the cakes, gently spreading with the back of a spoon so it reaches to the edges. Let set for 2–3 hours.

Divide the fondant into thirds and color one portion pale pink (see page 11). Seal in a plastic bag at room temperature. Repeat with the remaining fondant, coloring one portion pale blue and the other pale yellow. Roll out to about 1/8" thick on a board sprinkled with confectioners' sugar. Stamp out the blossoms and butterflies and let them dry for a few hours. It is best to prop up the butterflies' wings with chopsticks or pencils as they dry, so they set as if in flight.

Using the royal icing, stick the blossoms and butterflies to the cakes. Be quite random, so each cake is unique. As a final touch, pipe dots on to each cake and centers into every blossom. Arrange on a cake stand.

MAKES ABOUT 80

Very Lemony Crunch Cake batter (page 31)

80 ovenproof foil candy liners
4¾ cups confectioners' sugar, plus more for rolling
5–6 tablespoons fresh lemon juice
blue food coloring
yellow food coloring
pink (or red) food coloring
3½ ounces white fondant
¼", ½", and ¾" blossom cutters
¾"-wide butterfly cutter
¼ cup white royal icing, in a parchment paper cone (see page 9)

christmas gifts

These are perfect as a token edible gift, especially for someone living alone, or for Christmas fairs or teachers' presents. Cut little square gifts from a large cake if you prefer, but here I cook them in aluminum food cans. (You can also bake them in muffin pans, but be sure to line them with parchment paper.) The batter comes to no harm waiting around for an hour or 2, as it will probably need to be cooked in batches.

Butter each can well, then line the bottoms and sides very carefully with parchment paper. Make sure you leave 1" of parchment higher than the sides of the can to make the cakes easier to remove.

Preheat the oven to 275°F. Fill each can with about $1/3$ cup of the batter and place them on baking sheets. Bake for 45–50 minutes or until a wooden toothpick inserted into the center comes out clean. Let cool for 15 minutes. Turn out on to a wire rack and cool completely. Sprinkle each cake with a little of the rum.

Bring the jam and rum for glazing to a boil in a small saucepan, then rub through a sieve. Dab a little into the center of each board. Place a cake on each, then brush a little more glaze all over the tops and sides.

Sprinkle a rolling pin and work surface with confectioners' sugar and roll out about $31/2$ ounces of marzipan to $1/4$" thick. Lift on to a cake, gently press it to the sides, then cut away the excess. It's important that the marzipan comes right down to the board all around the cake to seal in moisture. Repeat until all the cakes are covered. Let dry overnight.

Cut 12" lengths of ribbon and wrap around some of the cakes, glueing in place at the back with a little royal icing. Twist raffia around other cakes and tie with a knot.

It is more fun to decorate each cake slightly differently, using a sprig of artificial berries, cinnamon sticks, dried orange slices, or star anise flowers. Use the royal icing to glue them into place. Tie up the little cakes in individual cellophane bags (see page 202) - or a piece of cellophane cut from a sheet - and finish with a ribbon or a gift tag.

MAKES 22

Tropical Fruit Cake batter
(page 44)

22 (15-ounce) aluminum food
  cans
butter, for the cans
$2/3$ cup apricot jam
3 tablespoons rum, plus 7
  tablespoons for the glaze
Twenty-two 4" diameter rounds,
  cut from thin cake cardboard
confectioners' sugar, for rolling
2 recipes marzipan (see page
  138) (or 4 pounds store-bought
  marzipan)
7 yards ribbons or raffia
$1/3$ cup royal icing in a parchment
  paper cone (see page 9)
selection of artificial berries,
  cinnamon sticks, dried orange
  slices, and star anise flowers

melting snowmen

Not everyone wants to eat fruit cake at Christmas, and these are simple enough for children to decorate.

Line 20 muffin cups with foil cupcake liners. Pack the cake mixture into the cups so that each is slightly domed. Place in the refrigerator to set.

Divide the royal icing between 3 small bowls. Leave 1 bowl of icing white, and tint the second bowl black and the third bowl red. Transfer each icing to a parchment paper cone (see page 9).

To make the snowmen's heads, roll 20 balls of fondant (each about the size of a cherry). Sprinkle a work top and rolling pin with confectioners' sugar and roll out the remaining fondant to ¼" thick. Using the cutter, cut out 20 circles. Place 1 on to each cake and smooth into place. Using the white royal icing, stick a snowman's head on to each cake. Let dry for a few hours.

Pipe 2 black eyes and a red nose on to each snowman, then stick on 2 miniature candy buttons. Finish by twisting a length of candy around the neck of each snowman, holding in place with a little more royal icing.

MAKES 20 FAIRY CAKES

Surprise Icebox Cake mixture
  (page 56)

20 foil cupcake liners
½ cup royal icing (see page 9)
black food coloring paste
red food coloring paste
1¼ pounds white fondant
confectioners' sugar, for rolling
2¼" round cookie cutter
40 miniature sugar-coated
  chocolate candies
assorted strands, laces and long
  striped candies

fruit-and-nut cupcakes

A batch of these make a lovely display on a cake stand at Christmas, or packed into a box as a gift and wrapped in ribbon. They're also vegan.

Preheat the oven to 275°F. Line 34 muffin cups in 3 muffin pans with the liners (or bake in batches). Divide the cake mixture between them. Bake for about 1 hour, or until they spring back to the touch. Transfer to a wire rack and let cool.

Gently warm the jam in a small saucepan, then rub through a sieve. Brush it over the cakes. Decorate each cake with 3 pecans, 4 almonds and 4 half-cherries. Place the confectioners' sugar in a bowl and gradually add the rum, until you achieve a piping consistency, adding 1 teaspoon water if necessary. Place in the pastry bag, snip the end and drizzle over the cakes.

Arrange on a cake stand or pack into a gift box.

MAKES 34

Vegan Fruit Cake batter (page 52)

34 paper cupcake paper liners
$2/3$ cup apricot jam
102 pecans
136 whole blanched almonds
68 glacé cherries, halved
$1\frac{1}{4}$ cups confectioners' sugar, sifted
3 tablespoons rum
disposable pastry bag

cookies

iced, layered shortbread

Try lots of fillings. Why not lemon curd, chocolate nut spread, or dulce de leche? The cut-out centers in different shapes could be turned into mini cookies, or re-rolled.

Preheat the oven to 350°F.

On a floured board, roll the dough out to about ⅛" thick. Using the 2½" cutter, cut out 40 shortbreads. Using the 1" round cutter (or the heart, star, or blossom cutters, if you wish), cut a hole in the centers of half of the cookies. If they are to be frozen, lay the unbaked cookies between sheets of parchment paper in an airtight container. Defrost for 1 hour before baking.

Arrange the shortbreads on 2 large baking sheets lined with parchment paper. Cook for 12–15 minutes. Cool a few minutes on the baking sheets. Carefully transfer to a wire rack and cool completely.

Drizzle the royal icing back and forth over the surfaces of the cookies with the cut-out centres. Let the icing dry.

Spread your chosen filling on all the whole shortbreads. Sandwich together with the iced top layers.

MAKES 20 COOKIES

Classic Shortbread dough
  (page 74)

all-purpose flour, for rolling
2½" and 1" round cookie cutters
1" heart cookie cutter (optional)
1" star cookie cutter (optional)
1" blossom cookie cutter
  (optional)
¼ cup royal icing in a parchment
  paper cone (see page 9)
2 teaspoons per cookie
  strawberry jam, chocolate
  spread, lemon curd, or dulce
  de leche

doily cookies

Paper doilies appeared many, many years ago as a cheaper alternative to the crocheted linen used by the aristocracy as far back as the 17th century. By the 1950s, they had become a symbol of upward mobility; no ladies' gathering with the vicar would be complete without them! With our current interest in all things retro, they have found a resurgence. These are fun to make; use the tiniest cutters you can find.

Roll out the dough to about $\frac{1}{8}$" thick. It is quite sticky, so sprinkle both the work top and rolling pin with flour and chill the dough every now and then to firm up if necessary. Once rolled, refrigerate before cutting out shapes. Cut out 30 heart shapes. At this point, you could layer the cookies very carefully between parchment paper in an airtight container and freeze. Defrost for 1 hour before baking.

When ready to bake, preheat the oven to 350°F. Arrange the cookies on baking sheets lined with parchment paper. Cut shapes from each with the aspic cutters. Using a thin bamboo skewer, pierce tiny holes in the cookies to form a pattern you like.

Bake for 12–15 minutes until pale gold. Cool on the trays for a few minutes. Very carefully transfer them to a wire rack. They will firm up as they cool. Display on a plate or cake stand (with or without a paper doily!).

MAKES 30

Vanilla Butter Cookies dough
  (page 76)

all-purpose flour, for rolling
3" heart cookie cutter
tiny aspic cutters

easter tree cookies

Hang these rabbits, eggs and chicks on a few branches of spring blossom for an instant edible display. Children will enjoy decorating these…and not a chocolate egg in sight!

Preheat the oven to 350°F. Roll out the dough using plenty of flour (it is quite sticky) to about ⅛" thick. Cut out the cookies with your chosen cutters and arrange on 2 baking sheets lined with parchment paper. Make holes towards the top of each with a skewer for threading the ribbon. Bake for 12–15 minutes, or until pale gold. Cool on the baking sheets for a few minutes. Carefully transfer to a wire rack, re-forming the ribbon holes with the skewer, and cool completely.

Divide the fondant into 3 and place in separate plastic bags. Leave one white for the rabbits, color one pale yellow for the chicks and the other pale green for the eggs (see page 11).

Divide the royal icing between 3 small bowls. Leave 1 bowl of icing white. Tint the second bowl of icing pink, and the third bowl yellow. Transfer each icing to a parchment paper cone (see page 9).

On a clean work surface sprinkled with confectioners' sugar, roll out the white fondant to a little less than ⅛" thick. Cut out with the rabbit cutter, making as many as you have rabbit cookies. Pipe a little royal icing on to the cookie and stick on the fondant rabbit. Make a hole in the fondant in the same place as that on the cookie for the ribbon. Repeat with the yellow fondant on the chicks and the green for the eggs. Pipe pink dots on the rabbit, an ear and an eye, a pink eye for the chick and yellow patterns on the egg.

Let the fondant and icing set overnight. Cut the ribbons into 10" lengths and thread through each cookie.

MAKES 24

Vanilla Butter Cookies dough (page 76)

all-purpose flour, for rolling
selection of cookie cutters (I used a rabbit, an egg and a chick, each about 2½" long)
1½ pounds white fondant
yellow food coloring paste
green food coloring paste
1 cup royal icing (see page 9)
pink food coloring paste
confectioners' sugar, for rolling
2 yards ¼" wide lilac gingham ribbon
2 yards ¼" wide orange gingham ribbon
2 yards ¼" wide pink gingham ribbon

autumn leaves

Damp mists, woolly sweaters, and long strolls gathering horse chestnuts, meandering through the rustling leaves: each year I wait in anticipation for this time of year, but you can bake these whenever you want. Leaf shapes are very forgiving to make without a cutter. While there are leaf cookie cutters available, their shapes aren't very natural, so I made a template with plastic. These are perfect with a hot cup of tea or cider following a brisk stroll.

Roll out the dough on a lightly floured surface to about $1/4$" thick. Refrigerate on baking sheets for 30 minutes; this makes it far easier to cut. Cut through the dough around the leaf templates with a sharp knife. With the knife tip, score the veins of the leaves. Place on baking sheets lined with parchment paper. Preheat the oven to 350°F. If the dough softens before you get to it, refrigerate to firm it up again. (If it's too soft, it will be impossible to cut.)

Bake for 10–15 minutes; the cookies will have darkened a little. Let cool on the sheets for a few minutes, then transfer to a wire rack to cool completely. They will become crisp.

Using the brush, lightly dust the leaves with a little gold powder.

MAKES 30-40

Gingerbread Cookies dough
  (page 73)

all-purpose flour, for rolling
plastic or cardboard stencils of
  leaves (each about 3" long), or
  leaf cookie cutters
small paint brush
edible gold powder

stained glass
tree cookies

These look stunning on a Christmas tree; the colored "glass"
glows when lit by lights or candles. The cookies only last
a few days on a tree, so eat them before they soften. Use
whatever seasonal cookie cutters you have, though you will
need 2 sizes of each shape.

Preheat the oven to 350°F. Place all the candies of the same color in a
plastic bag, and crush finely by smashing with a rolling pin. Discard
the wrappers. Line 2 baking sheets with parchment paper.

Roll out the dough on a lightly floured surface to about ¼" thick.
Cut out your chosen shapes with the larger cutters. Using the smaller
cutters, cut the appropriate shape out of the middle of each cookie.
Pierce a hole with a skewer to thread a ribbon later. Where you make
the hole is important as it will affect the way the cookie hangs from
the tree. Re-roll the dough and repeat until it's all used up. (You may
need to refrigerate the dough if it gets too soft during this process.)
Bake for about 5 minutes, then remove from the oven.

Fill the central hole in each cookie with the crushed candies. Re-form
the ribbon hole if necessary. Return the cookies to the oven and bake
for a further 5–10 minutes. Remove from the oven and re-form the
ribbon holes for a final time. Cool completely on the baking sheets.

Cut the ribbon into 10" lengths and thread through each cookie.

MAKES ABOUT 20

Gingerbread Cookies dough
(page 73)

15–20 hard candies, such as
sour balls
all-purpose flour, for rolling
3½" and 1½" heart cookie cutters
4½" and 1½" tree cookie cutters
4" and 1½" angel cookie cutters
5" and 2" snowflake cookie
cutters
6½ yards narrow ribbon

gingerbread mobile

A magical addition to any child's room, or anywhere for that matter. The gingerbreads could be any shape: snowflakes or stars at Christmas, butterflies, hearts, flowers, or animals. Use whatever cutters you have, or draw a template.

Preheat the oven to 350°F. Line a baking sheet with parchment paper. Chill the dough, then roll it out to about ¼" thick on a lightly floured surface. Cut out the birds and pierce a hole in each with a skewer to thread the ribbon later. Where you make the hole is important as it will affect the way the bird hangs. Press in a dragee eye for each bird. Bake for 10–15 minutes. Remove from the oven and re-form the holes with the skewer. Leave to firm up for a few minutes, then transfer to a wire rack to cool. They will become crisp. When cool, stick a dragee eye on to the reverse side of each bird, using a little royal icing.

For the mobile, wind the wider ribbon round and round the hoop, overlapping and securing with a firm knot on the inside of the ring. Wrap the cardboard ring with ribbon too, and tie in the same way.

Cut the remaining wide ribbon into 4 equal lengths. Thread the end of 1 piece through a button and tie it around the hoop with a knot. Repeat with the other 3 lengths of ribbon and 3 more buttons, spacing them out evenly around the hoop. Take the other ends of these 4 ribbons and thread them through the cardboard ring, then through the final button. Knot off neatly.

Take 2 feet of the narrow ribbon and loop it, too, through the top button. This will hang the mobile.

Thread more of the narrow ribbon through each gingerbread bird. Hang 2 from the cardboard ring and 5 from the embroidery hoop. Hang up the mobile from the central ribbon.

MAKES 15 OR 20 BIRDS;
7 BIRDS MAKE 1 MOBILE

½ recipe Gingerbread Cookies
  dough (page 73)

all-purpose flour, for rolling
dove cookie cutter (or template)
swallow cookie cutter (or
  template)
14 green dragees
2 tablespoons royal icing in a
  parchment paper cone (see
  page 9)
reel of ¾" wide orange ribbon
8" embroidery hoop
1 cardboard ring from a roll
  of cellophane tape
5 green buttons with large slots
  or holes
reel of ¼" wide orange ribbon

25 easy cheats

Almost anything can be a decoration, so make a collection of items as you find them.

1 candles
There is a wonderful selection of candles and candleholders available. And try small votive candles or tea lights, too. A cake studded with many different, carefully selected candles looks stunning.

Take special care with candles on cakes as they need to be placed well away from other decorations, especially ribbons or artificial flowers.

2 tea lights
Place in a scooped-out clementine, or make a collar out of fondant. I once made a simple crown with cut-out stars in fondant, shaped into a short cylinder. This went on top of the cake with a tea light in the middle. It glowed in the dark.

3 the supermarket shelf
There's no need solely to rely on mail order specialists; be creative with the plethora of goods you'll find in local shops. I found tiny sugar dragees, piped sugar flowers, crystallized rose and violet petals and little sugar orange and lemon slices.

4 fresh flowers
Choose your favorites and be absolutely sure they are edible before placing on the cake. You can paint the edges of the petals with egg white and dip into clear or colored glitter (I love to do this with white or deep red roses at Christmas). Place 3 or 5 (they always look better when you use an odd number) of glittering roses on a large cake – it looks amazing.

5 bright paper flowers
It is child's play to make tissue or crêpe paper flowers. Stick a circle of them on top of a cake.

6 fresh berries and fruit
For an instant, wonderful decoration, paint them with egg white and dip into superfine sugar to crystallize (see page 107). The addition of a few appropriate leaves - try mint with berries, or bay leaves in winter - adds real impact.

7 candies and chocolates
Make patterns with them or limit the color palette; using simply black and white, or red and white. Try monochrome licorice, black-and-white striped ribbon, and a red candle.

8 ribbons, braids, and beading
Ribbons are instant decorations and most effective. Wrap them around a cake, layer them, overlay different colors, or pull them into a flower shape.

9 doilies and stencils
A visit to your local cake shop will reveal all sorts. I especially like to use heart-shaped doilies on a heart-shaped cake. On the surface of a very flat cake, place a doily or a stencil (make one yourself, maybe the initials of the recipient) and dust with confectioners' sugar or cocoa powder. Very carefully remove the overlay to reveal an intricate pattern.

10 pile of tiny parcels
Cover little matchboxes with plain or tiny-patterned wrapping paper. Tie them with narrow ribbons and decorate with miniature decorations; try bows or flowers. Pile them on a birthday or Christmas cake.

11 reuse packaging
Keep little boxes, bags, ribbons, tissue paper, even the cellophane bags from greetings cards. Use to package home-made cookies or little cakes.

12 button cookies
Use any of my cookie recipes to make little round cookies. Pierce 2 or 4 holes in the middle of the raw cookies to resemble buttonholes, then bake, re-form the holes when they come out of the oven and tie licorice laces or ribbons through the holes.

13 parcels
A square cake can be an edible gift. Wrap the recipient's favorite cake in fondant. Transform into "wrapping paper" by drawing with edible pens or food coloring, or stick on candies, sugar flowers or dragees. For Christmas, draw on holly and stick on stars. Tie with ribbon and add a hand-written tag.

14 no time to bake?

Dress up a bakery cake. If you buy a plain cake, make flavored buttercream (see page 9) and layer it or simply spread on top. Decorate with any of the quick ideas on this page. If you buy a fruit cake, add a little liqueur (brandy, rum, or Madeira), then decorate with ribbon and fresh flowers. Or buy lots of cupcakes, ice with buttercream and pile on an array of candies. Kids would love to make these.

15 buy yourself some time

Keep children quiet for a while by getting them to make small cakes into "bugs." Give them some multi-colored chocolate candies and tubes of colored icing from the supermarket. They can make bodies with the candies and pipe on legs and faces.

16 mind the gap

If someone has pinched a slice from a whole cake (especially if it was you), disguise the crime. Slice all the cake, space the slices out and top each with a decoration, or cover each slice with glacé icing.

17 edible pens

A marvelous invention available at baking suppliers. Draw anything on a fondant-coated cake, from simple patterns to intricate pictures, in a range of colors. Make sure the fondant is dry first; leave it for at least 24 hours.

christmas quick fixes

18 decorative lights

Instantly enliven a cake with a set of widely available battery-operated Christmas lights. Twist them around the side of a cake, or among crystallized fruits or red berries.

19 make a relief

Cover the cake in marzipan and icing and let dry overnight. Then take a cutter of your choice - a large star or tree is very effective - and use it to cut through the icing layer. Remove the cut-out icing. Brush the exposed marzipan with melted apricot preserves and fill the shape with tiny dragees.

20 seasonal flowers

Cut a styrofoam cup down by half, fill with a piece of moistened fibral foam and pack in holly and berry sprigs (obviously poisonous, so don't let anyone try to eat them!) and other seasonal leaves to make a dramatic arrangement. Dust heavily with confectioners' sugar "snow" and finish with a sprinkle of clear glitter.

21 votive candles

Arrange a thick, stubby, unscented votive candle, a fresh full-blown red rose and a bundle of cinnamon sticks tied up with strands of raffia on top of a plain white iced cake.

22 decorate with candies

Make a stocking, star or tree shape with small candies, such as miniature chocolate buttons or jelly beans. Be inspired by my Mosaic Cake (page 90).

23 crystallized fruits

These are widely available during the festive period. Take a fruit cake covered in marzipan - or fully iced if you prefer - and make a pile of crystallized fruits in the center. Tuck in a few fresh bay leaves (warn your guests these are inedible!) and, if you like, add a touch of gold leaf to the leaves (see page 68), slightly dampening the leaves by sprinkling with a little water first.

24 artificial berries

Take branches of red berries and twist them into a circle the same diameter as a plain white iced cake. Place the wreath on the cake and finish with a broad, deep red ribbon.

25 gingerbread cutters

Buy a few cutters - maybe a gingerbread man, a heart, a tree, or star - and use them to make a batch of my Gingerbread Cookies (page 73). Wash the cutters and layer 3 or 4 of the cookies inside. Place into a bag (see tip 11, opposite) with a hand-written copy of the recipe, and tie with ribbon.

index

suppliers list

cake and sugarcraft products, including food coloring pastes, cake cardboards and drums, bulk fondant, and marzipan
www.thebakerskitchen.com
(419) 381-9693

www.shopbakersnook.com
(734) 429-1320

www.sugarcraft.com
(513) 896-7089 (no phone orders)

candies, including flower lollipops
www.twinklecandy.com
online only

candies, including twin cherry lollipops
www.4greatcandy.com
online only

candy molds (Easter eggs)
www.candymoldcentral.com
(309) 747-2844 (no phone orders)

floral picks, feathers, artificial flowers and birds
www.save-on-crafts.com
(831) 768-8428

gold leaf
www.ediblegold.com
(415) 407-5097

pearl spray
www.consumercrafts.com
(888) 55-CRAFT

raffia
www.bjcraftsupplies.com
(361) 286-3719

ribbons and braids
www.mjtrim.com
(800) 9-MJTRIM

credits
page 23 pink floral fabric, page 25 floral fabric, page 29 blue-and-white-striped fabric, page 63 spotty and fine-stripe fabrics, page 70 colourful floral fabric, page 91 white embroidered fabric, page 142 white fabric on table, all Cloth House (www.clothhouse.co.uk); page 42 floral fabric (design: Mirande), page 83 floral fabric (design: Rosanna) and page 145 embroidered spot fabric (design: Carreg), all Sanderson (www.sanderson-uk.com); page 77 floral silk fabric (design: Rosamund Celadon), Designers Guild (www.designersguild. com); page 142 wallpaper (design: Mandara), Osborne & Little (www.osborneandlittle.com)

EDITORIAL DIRECTOR Anne Furniss
CREATIVE DIRECTOR Helen Lewis
PROJECT EDITOR Lucy Bannell
DESIGNER Claire Peters
PHOTOGRAPHER Laura Hynd
STYLIST Rachel Jones
PRODUCTION DIRECTOR Vincent Smith
PRODUCTION CONTROLLER Aysun Hughes

First published in 2010 by
Quadrille Publishing Limited
Alhambra House
27-31 Charing Cross Road
London WC2H 0LS
www.quadrille.co.uk

Mention of specific companies, organizations, or authorities in this book does not imply endorsement by the author or publisher, nor does mention of specific companies, organizations, or authorities imply that they endorse this book, its author, or the publisher.

Internet addresses and telephone numbers given in this book were accurate at the time it went to press.

Printed in China

Library of Congress Cataloging-in-Publication Data.

Cairns, Fiona.
  Bake & decorate: charming cakes, cupcakes & cookies for every occasion / Fiona Cairns
       p. cm.
  Includes index.
  ISBN-13 978-1-60529-204-5 hardcover
  ISBN-10 1-60529-204-4 hardcover
  1. Cake. 2. Cookies. 3. Cake decorating. I. Title.
TX771.C238 2010
641.8'6539—dc22   2010018466
Distributed to the trade by Macmillan
2 4 6 8 10 9 7 5 3 1 hardcover

RODALE

The word 'acknowledgment' seems so inadequate. Creating a book is a collective process, and I would like to thank so many people.

Firstly my agent Heather Holden-Brown and lovely Elly James for all your patience. Special thanks to Anne Furniss at Quadrille for your faith in me and giving me this amazing opportunity. To my gentle, encouraging editor Lucy Bannell, it has been a great privilege working with you. To Laura Hynd for beautiful, calming photographs. To Claire Peters for wonderful design and Rachel Jones for sensitive styling.

To my old friend Jacqui Pickles, the best cook I know, for your help with development of the most delicious recipes and your work on testing others. Thank you. Without your flair, advice and constructive criticism this book wouldn't be what it is.

To Rachel Eardley. Your talent is exceptional and your creativity knows no bounds. I cannot thank you enough for all your inspiration and help on the book, quite apart from filling in for me at work as well!

I would like to thank Chris Adams, my dear friend, baker and plantswoman extraordinaire. Thank you for your generosity, advice and help (most especially for your exquisite crystallized flowers).

No less gratitude goes to all at the Bakery, both past and present. We are blessed with an exceptional team led by Kishore. Special thanks to Mary Doody (your roses are the best!), Diane Pallett, Angela Withers and Kasia Skotnicka-Tkacz.

Anna Tyler. Your enthusiasm and sheer hard work in the kitchen has been extraordinary and has made this so much easier. I cannot thank you enough. To your wonderful mother Joan for all her recipe testing and wise comments, and to Kiki Everard, Amanda Taylor and Eleanor Kilpatrick. David Marshall-Cook and John Moore, thank you for creating Christmas and dappled light respectively! To David Trumper at Jane Asher and Jade Johnston at the Kitchen Range Cookshop in Market Harborough, for your patience. Many, many thanks to Marina Hill for her typing with such speed and efficiency.

I thank my mother for encouraging me to bake at a young age, with rather varying results! Thank you to Lyn Hall, who years ago set me on my way and first taught me the meaning of excellence.

Last, but most definitely not least, to Kishore for running the business so brilliantly and for being my most valued critic! And to my children, Hari and Tara, who endured months of disruption. Sometimes banned from the kitchen and (mostly) uncomplaining, this would not have been possible without you. Thank you.